# SMALL STATES.

# BIG POSSIBILITIES.

Why small states are simply better

Andreas Marquart and Philipp Bagus

Translator: Vanessa Walsh
Project Manager: Andrew Stover
Cover Design: Andrew Stover

# CONTENTS

# SPECIAL THANKS

*This translation would not have been possible without the generous help of these crowdfunding backers:*

## *Defenders of the Realm $30*

Steve Foerster

Mark Frazier
Chris DeMorro

*Lords of the Realm $100*
Ralph Martins Ernest Ortiz
Andrew Stover

*Emperor of the Realm $500*

Thibault Henri Serlet

*Additionally, special thanks to Vanessa Walsh for the translation and Andrew Stover for organizing the production of this English publication.*

# PREFACE

## By David Howden

## Small is the New Big

The last 30 years has culminated in several trends in the Western World. Some of these have been good and others decidedly less so. These trends have fallen under the broad umbrella of what is typically called "neoliberalism". Free trade reigns, the private sector has displaced the public in large swaths of most economies, government assets have been privatized and a general trend towards deregulation has flourished. While it is at times difficult to comprehend that the current status quo differs substantially from earlier periods, it is useful to consider just how much the modern world differs from the post-war period.

At the end of the Second World War, the top US tax rate was 94%. It remained over 70% through to the 1980s. Government owned businesses dominated most economies during this period. From oil to airlines to telecoms, the choices of the consumer basics that we take for granted today were severely curtailed.

Not all the changes have been for the better. While Western governments slowly devolved economic power to the private sector, they worked vigorously to centralize political might. The reunification of Germany in 1990 brought 16 million new Eastern subjects to the dominion of the Bonn government (or 63 million West Germans into the realm of Berlin, depending on how you look at it). The rise of the European Union and the centralized European superstate has continued relatively unabated. Indeed, one of the EU's must successful foreign policies has been its own enlargement.

At first glance this seems to be a good thing. After all, didn't various Western governments pursue the liberalizations that defined the past 30 year? We're 16 million East Germans made better off by being subjugated to a more market-friendly government in Western Germany?

What the government gives it just as easily takes away. We are now witnessing the early stages of the eruption that has been forming under these increasingly centralized states. The European separatist movements, in Catalonia, Scotland, Britain and elsewhere are being denied self-determination – not just by the national governments immediately responsible for these areas, but also by the EU. The average citizen is being overwhelmed by expansion fatigue, yet the bureaucrats in Brussels show no sign of tiring.

Such expansion of a centralized European state were unheard of just a few short decades ago. After all, we should not forget that Charles de Gaulle vetoed British membership to the EU in 1963, and François Mitterrand feared that allowing the dictatorships of Greece, Spain and Portugal would compromise the free-trade area.

If one admits that the last 30 years have been defined by economic liberalizations, one must also readily admit that this has coincided with the expansion and strengthening of the centralized state – both in theory and in practice.

The sun is setting on this period and the winds are blowing in a new paradigm. Free trade is under attack. Likewise, separatism and the desire for smaller political units is emerging. Until now the demand for smaller states has taken the form of an emotional backlash against homogenous one-size-fits-all policies. Regional governments, anxious to aggrandize themselves relative to their centralize superiors, have been all too happy to take up this secessionist causes.

What these various causes lack is a common theoretical core to understand why small is beautiful, and how a reduced state can provide for its people better than a large one. If the past 30 years engrained the idea that big states are superior to small ones, we need to formulate the theoretical core to convince people that small is the new big.

Europe is at a crossroads with two outcomes. One path is to federalize it into the "United States of Europe". Given the prevailing animosity projected by Europeans, from the smallest citizen to the highest reaches of government, towards the large-scale American domination of the world, there is some amount of dissonance surrounding this outcome. The alternative is to break up, and return to small political units and the doctrine of self-determination. This book shows the reader how it's feasible, and desirable.

# FOREWORD

By Roland Tichy

# Brexit, Trump's Deal and Europe

When Donald Trump, president-elect of the United States of America, announced new "Deals" for the US economy, the Euro and stock market prices in Europe, in part, fell sharply on the day of the declaration. Trump's words hit automobile companies harder than the Volkswagen diesel scandal. These aren't "book values". Stock markets are sensitive measurement systems for uncertainty and change. Do the Germans have to be afraid of Trump? What's happening to Europe, which is now passing through a phase of uncertainty and dispute over the future of its organization? Must Europe become more integrated? Is the United States of Europe now needed more urgently than ever? Is more centralization necessary to be able to develop sufficient political force against Trump?

Andreas Marquart and Philipp Bagus deal with these burning questions in their book We Can Do It Alone, and conclude that, contrary to popular opinions, Europe needs more decentralization and more political competition. For the authors, the answer to globalization lies in small political entities rather than giant states, which, as in the case of Trump's presidency, have the potential to cause great damage—like bulls in china shops. The Prince of Liechtenstein or the Swiss Federal President, on the other hand, don't use their tweets to move the stock market prices of this world, and that's a good thing. They don't possess the dangerous, unpredictable power that Trump wields.

The strange thing is that Trump fulfills what the Left and the Greens are longing for in Germany: he's slowing down globalization and ending economic liberalism. He rules the economy via Twitter and thus runs the opposite of a regulatory policy that separates business and politics. Berlin has long since become more and more deeply involved in the micro-network of the economy. What's more, Berlin has too much power. In the authors' eyes, even in the German nation state, too much power has been concentrated. Marquart and Bagus plead for even smaller political units, an unusual approach, but certainly one worth considering. After all, it would be easier for many small states to escape the directives of Berlin and to compete in freer areas. Competition sets policy limits.

Trump is doing what many in Germany want: he is enforcing the primacy of politics, and the economy has to follow his tweeted orders. U.S. companies began halting production relocations abroad: 1,000 jobs in a refrigeration factory in Indiana were rescued.

German cars, which are built cheaply in Mexico and imported from there to the USA, are to be charged with a 35 percent penalty tax. But the Germans had calculated well, and set out to supply the cheap industrial location of Mexico with willing workers from all over America, from Alaska to Tierra del Fuego, and part of Asia.

## Structural Change as a Prosperity Machine

Trump's 'New Deal' is a radical break from the post-war order of the economy. Germany hopped back on its feet after the Second World War, because the four-wheeled Volkswagen "bugs" from Wolfsburg were allowed to crawl through America and import money from there to help the "economic miracle".

The opening up of markets, first of all in the West, then, in the whole world after 1989, was a global economic recovery plan. It insisted that it would bring benefits to all those involved if the factories moved to where wages are still low. The textile industry did so: first the sewing shops moved to southern Europe, then to North Africa, later to China and finally to Bangladesh and Burma. Other industries followed the trend. Apple's products are invented in Silicon Valley, but are produced in China by Foxconn (with approximately 450,000 employees).

The classic industrialized countries are both winners and losers in globalization: they lose jobs in structural change and are constantly forced to create higher-quality jobs with new products and ideas until they, too, are lost again. Germany, as well, has had to give up important industries: in the production of household appliances, consumer electronics, cameras

—dramatic for the employees. And yet, the constant structural change and forced innovation became a powerful prosperity machine.

It's not only the opening up of the United States that has made Germany what it is today. The continuing process of unification in Europe has helped Germany. The opening up of Eastern Europe after the fall of the Iron Curtain accelerated the process of moving Germany back into the center of Europe. This process is fundamentally dependent on the fact that the borders remain open. It's politically questionable that Trump designates Europe as a German project for enforcing German interests, but economic data supports this idea. The Germans have made the best use of the opportunities offered by the common market and have repeatedly managed crises to their advantage.

## *Self-Sufficiency is Expensive and Usually Impossible*

Recently, however, discomfort with open markets has grown. Free trade agreements are rejected, and fair, i.e. higher prices for products from other countries, are promoted for ethical reasons. Global standards for working conditions are created with the intent to slow down the global cycle. This also applies to Europe where open markets are seen by many as a similar threat. For example, when it comes to agriculture, the German dairy farmers would like to abolish Europe for themselves. Calls for public tender or procurement which must span all of Europe burden municipalities.

At the beginning of the post-war boom, however, the huge US market opened for Europeans. Germany was the winner from the beginning and, if you will, a perpetrator of globalization, not a victim. Of all major countries, the German economic system is the most precisely targeted. Cheap supply from the factories of Eastern Europe, then domestic processing and, finally, expensive export to the world markets. Global integration and supply chains right down to the tightest corner. That's the German model!

It's a successful model because it has been able to assert itself against protectionist advances - especially China which is always starting new attempts to unilaterally change the rules to its advantage. If Donald Trump actually goes through with his "New Deal", Germany must reinvent itself.

Trump names the USA as a loser. It has opened its markets and millions of jobs have been lost. However, not only in Europe, but especially in Asia, hundreds of millions of people have escaped poverty; new middle classes have emerged. Trump claims that this has happened at the expense of America. Is that fair?

Protectionism is harmful to all parties involved. However, Marquart and Bagus demonstrate convincingly that large economies are better able to deal with protectionism because they can maintain division of labor and specialization within their borders, at least in moderation. Smaller, specialized economies literally starve outside the door. This is the clear lesson from the interwar period. After the global free trade movement was frozen, great empires like the Ottoman Empire, the Austro-Hungarian Empire, the Russian Tsarist Empire and the German Empire disintegrated into smaller and smaller units that were isolated from each other. Self-sufficiency is an expensive, usually even impossible solution that creates conflicts, which, as history teaches, are often carried out in a bloody manner.

Competitive pressure and citizens with close proximity, as the authors show, have many advantages. Smaller countries are usually better managed and more imaginative in their social development. In any case, they tend to be less aggressive. In order to replace the lack of economies of scale, common economic areas have been invented in the past without foreclosure and trade barriers. That was the birth of the EU. It goes hand in hand with high growth rates.

That's why Germany needs Europe. The question is: does it need *this* Europe? Does it need further political centralization? Does the demand for more and more protectionism not trigger and deepen conflicts? Are there other forms of cooperation that are less cumbersome because they require less dramatic change? In this book, the authors search for such answers. Europe needs the competition of ideas such as that which takes place between its regions. This competition, Marquart and Bagus argue, has excelled and magnified Europe. Could it not be the case that a Europe consisting of only decentralized and flexible small units may provide the right answer to the threat of protectionism?

## *Trump Fulfills Wishes from the Greens and the Left*

Trump calls for a new profit mechanism (such as burden sharing) as well as for new security arrangements. Here, too, Germany has a weak point: it was living well under the American umbrella, and it was easy to criticize the defensive measures of the US from a position of pacifism. This attitude has suddenly been overtaken by "America First".

If you will, the liberal post-war era will end with Trump. Economic liberalism is not his business. The "real" Trump is what the Left and the Greens want: the end of globalization, the end of what could be called very general neo-liberalism. And regulatory policy? A tweet is enough to smash proven rules of power separation. Protectionism receives a new quality. "Prosperity for all" was thought of and formulated under a different sign.

Brexit is interpreted as a clever measure to escape the "German" Europe. If the British were initially considered "stupid" because they didn't want to continue to live with the blessings of the EU for themselves, they're now the "smart" ones. This message will also come to be understood in other

European countries. Trump is giving new energy to centrifugal forces in Europe. However, the answer cannot be "continue as we have before", but will instead require flexible answers.

# INTRODUCTION

*There is no alternative to Europe's political integration. Peace and prosperity for Germany is only ensured with this concept. The EU is the guarantor of Europe's position in the globalized world.*

These sentences are generally accepted. These promises of salvation have been the basis of German politics and media reporting for decades. They have been deeply embedded in our consciousness and self-image and have no longer become a questioned public opinion. Or have you ever questioned these statements? If not, then it's time. This is a matter which needs the kind of intellectual honesty and independent thinking which are at the root of every responsible action. And if German politics and public opinion are based on principles that, when viewed more closely, could turn out to be wrong, then we could be wandering down a disastrous path. Repentance would be required as soon as possible.

In this book, we want to shake up the aforementioned sentences and get to the bottom of their truthfulness.

There is reason enough, and time is of the essence. The decision of the British, on June 23rd, 2016, to leave the EU is undoubtedly a turning point against the efforts of European power elites to further integrate Europe.

The EU's gains in prosperity have also suffered some serious ruptures. The financial crisis, which erupted in 2008 with full force across the world and Europe, and the sluggish recovery, have caused a severe slump in the general enthusiasm for an even greater Europe.

Meanwhile, the political viewpoint defined by the italicized sentences that began this chapter seeks salvation in a broader political integration. In order to stabilize the European Monetary Community, people of this persuasion believe political union must immediately follow, and rules, regulations, and laws must be further harmonized. Ultimately, one can make a virtue out of necessity and, through the needs of this crisis achieve the dream of a political and economic union of European nation states more quickly. The challenges of globalization would present the individual states with ever greater hurdles, which could only be mastered together, not to mention the global war against terror and the management of the refugee crisis. And those who speak out against the EU even risk peace in Europe.

Eurocentrics use their arguments to determine public perception. But what about the quality of their arguments? Can they really convince people with an understandable and above all logical approach? Is "bigger" really automatically "better" in times of globalization? Would the emergence of Germany into the United States of Europe be a step forward? Would the EU state secure peace, freedom and prosperity? Are the interests of the Brussels power apparatus, including those of national governments, at all compatible with the interests of the citizens, or must the interests of both sides, by definition, have to be diametrically opposed? After all, the relationship between the citizen and the state is not voluntary.

While politics moves forward, it leaves more and more citizens behind, and they are beginning to doubt whether they want to go along the road that has been chosen from Brussels. This is due in no small part to the obvious surge that EU-critical political parties are now experiencing across Europe. The so-called people's parties and the leading media outlets, among the institutions most highly financed by compulsory public law, still manage to discredit those who wish to pull the brakes on the journey to the single European state as a supposed right-wing populist. Those who don't want to run the risk of being a Nationalist or Populist must support the EU single state or remain silent. This leads to a ban on thinking. The political Elite is in agreement: the EU single state must and will come. For this purpose, politicians, who are either conservative or Social-Democrat, once somewhat distinct, dilute their goals and ally themselves against the forces threatening their power and goals. The parties are becoming more and more indeterminate. Why this unity? Are the arguments for political centralization really so clear?

Not at all. The skepticism of the citizens is, as this book will point out, quite appropriate. Many people say their gut feeling tells them that something is heading in a completely wrong direction. They want to critically question the italicized statements made at the beginning of this chapter. The only thing they lack is the factual arguments needed to be able to stand up to politics and its propaganda machine. With this book, we want to give these arguments to the people not only in light of the Euro crisis and Brexit, but also so that they can succeed in taking the wind out of the sails of those who advocate for a unified European state. Despite the present weakening of those who are in favor of a single state, we are at a crossroads. Single state advocates want to continue their path undisturbed, or, if possible, at an even faster pace than before. Where it will lead is ultimately decided by the power of arguments. We hope to make a modest contribution here.

We will argue that the size of political structures is the deciding factor as to whether future or present generations will live in prosperity or poverty, freedom or bondage, peace or war.

EU advocates will be appalled, and even EU opponents may be surprised if our analyses show that achieving a desirable future will be achieved with neither a full-stop nor a reversal of the European integration process. For consistent thinking will only find its logical end within ever smaller political units. Please follow our unconventional direction of thought and you will never look at the EU and its integration consensus with the same eyes again. We promise. It may even be very easy for you, because our point of view is that of the individual, which is all too human. And it is precisely individuals who are placed at the center of our book and whom politics has for a long time lost sight of in the pursuit of ever greater political structures and more and more power.

When reading, please rid yourself of all mental barriers. Historically, national borders have always been subject to change, mostly unfortunately only as a result of victory or defeat in wars. However, borders can also be redrawn peacefully. The Union between Sweden and Norway dissolved by mutual consent in 1905. Similarly, the canton of Jura separated from the canton of Bern in 1979. Czechoslovakia was also peacefully divided in 1992.

Even the most totalitarian state the world has ever seen, the Soviet Union, dissolved without war into a variety of new states. Does this mean the peaceful emergence of new small states is a utopia? No way. Ultimately, it depends only on the people themselves. To end wars, John Lennon once said, "War is over, if you want it." He was of the opinion that as long as people had the idea of having no power, they would have no power. In variation of
Lennon's sentence: "Small states are possible, if you want them."

# WHY BREXIT COULD BE THE BEGINNING OF THE END OF THE EU

*It is very difficult for an economist to be a good European and at the same time to have the reputation of a good European.*

Wilhelm Röpke

# THE DRUMBEAT

It's Friday June 24th, 2016. People in Europe turn on their TVs or smartphones at breakfast, and they're utterly shocked. A nervous energy fills the air. The day before, contrary to all forecasts, the majority of British people voted to leave the European Union. Since the murder of Labour MP and EU advocate Jo Cox on June 16th, 2012, all polls indicated a victory for the EU camp. The British decided differently. Back to the 24th. The financial markets go crazy. The European stock markets are dropping fast. However, the shock and panic will soon turn out to be exaggerated. The stock market losses will be offset in just a few weeks.

The Brexit decision undoubtedly meant a cut through the post-Second World War history of European integration. The democratic choice of the British shocked the political elites, as well as the majority of the opinion forming media. The result was a huge blow to them. It questioned the dogma of an "ever closer union", an ever stricter unification in Europe. In fact, the ultimate goal of a political Union in Europe remains practically unquestioned by anyone in the political and media Elite. The "European agreement" is, at least when it was signed on December 23rd, 1999, a one-way street that would lead to a European state: the United States of Europe, to which, as spoken in Merkel's German, there was "no alternative" in the long term.

Shortly thereafter, the follow-up came for all who called themselves staunch Europeans. Nigel Farage, one of Brexit's best-known advocates, resigned as party leader of the United Kingdom Independence Party (UKIP) on July 4th, 2016. He had achieved the goal for which he co-founded UKIP 23 years ago and wanted his private life back. Influencers and celebrities like Christoph Waltz soon tried to compare him to a rat, which abandons the sinking ship. They missed the fact that Farage didn't even sit in the British Parliament as UKIP chief and had no chance of becoming Prime Minister. Only three UKIP members were present in parliament anyway. The leading role in carrying out Brexit was clearly attributed to the largest party in Westminster, the Conservatives (243 members).

Perhaps Waltz and some politicians simply couldn't bear Farage to behave so differently from ordinary politicians. He didn't stick to power. Unlike many professional politicians who stay in the spotlight and who blindly follow the party strategy, always seeking new tasks, Farage has principles and is consistent. He had achieved his goal and was able to leave politics behind.

# EUROCENTRIC ANXIETY

The political elites' response to Brexit came in a rush. Chancellor Merkel refused to tolerate cherry picking; a country could not secure only benefits. She said that if one wanted to have access to the internal market, they must also make commitments.

That sounded like barriers. While the EU was negotiating free trade agreements with Canada and the US at the same time, British access to the internal market was to be hampered as a penalty for the Brexit decision.

In the process, Merkel overlooked—or accepted approvingly—the fact that she harmed the German people with trade barriers, such as punitive tariffs. Free trade is an advantage for all parties who want to trade and negotiate. Punitive duties would make imports from the UK more expensive for EU consumers. Why did Merkel want to punish consumers in Germany and the EU? Just because the British voted for Brexit?

The situation is similar to that of a couple of siblings, in which the sister decides to move out of her brother's house, because he imposes new and overwhelming rules on her life. But the sister wants to maintain contact with him and the other family members. She wants to exchange with him and her nieces and nephews just as intimately as she did before. She just doesn't like the bureaucratic rules. The enraged brother shot back that this was cherry-picking. If she wanted to maintain contact with her nieces and nephews, she would have to be regulated and pay him a sum of money. He forbids his children from talking to their aunt. That this infantile behavior is to the detriment of everyone is obvious. Similarly, penalties and other barriers to British goods would damage European consumers.

The British side made it clear from the beginning that it was interested in free trade. After Brexit, Nigel Farage, who had never made a secret of his aversion to the bureaucratic monster in Brussels, appealed to EU politicians: "why don't we behave like adults, pragmatic, reasonable, realistic? Let us have a reasonable free-trade agreement to negotiate and then recognize that the United Kingdom will be your friend, that we will act with you, we will cooperate with you, we will be your best friends in the world."

# THE EU IS NOT EUROPE

Was the British vote an expression of anti-European tendencies? Let us ask more fundamentally: what is Europe doing? What helped Europe and Western culture take the lead in the world? What distinguishes Europe from other cultures?

The most important value of European culture is individual freedom. Nowhere else in the world could property rights and freedom prosper so well. Through this freedom, the Industrial Revolution overcame mass poverty in a politically fragmented Europe for the first time. This liberal fragmentation also gave rise to a variety of characteristics in Europe. And from this Europe, musical, artistic, literary and scientific innovations appeared that changed the whole world.

The sociologist Erich Weede describes the relationship between freedom and European fragmentation as follows: "For centuries, in contrast to Chinese history in particular, there has been a system of independent principalities, kingdoms or states that are independent of each other, capable of war and rivaling one another. The political fragmentation of Europe is crucial for the *relatively* liberal nature of Europe and its rise, while politically united China developed more slowly, even though it was still more economically and technologically advanced than Europe in the Middle Ages."

The historian Ralph Raico (1936-2016) came to a similar conclusion in his essay, *The European Miracle*: "Although geographical factors played a role and although Europe constituted itself as a single civilization—that of Roman Christianity—its radical decentralization is the key to Western development. Quite the contrary to other cultures, especially China, India and the Islamic world, Europe was a system of divided and, therefore, competing powers and legal systems."

Huge realms, such as those created and still existing in Asia, cause political errors to pile up and remain uncorrected. The philosopher Karl Popper (1902-1994) said: "Any accumulation of political power leads to the need for small errors to remain unnoticed at first..." But it isn't only a matter of reducing errors and failures as quickly as possible. In general, in small states, the effects of poor policies are more quickly and directly visible. From a moral point of view, it's much more difficult that the high concentration of power in huge empires will lead to individual freedom. And without freedom, technological, cultural and economic progress will be halted. Europe's rise and prosperity is therefore inextricably linked to its political decentralization.

# AN UN-EUROPEAN EU

It seems that with the centralization of power in Brussels and their dogma of an "ever closer union", EU politicians are working towards the goal of a new giant empire. Europe would become unfaithful to its history and become a new China. The EU elites actually regard this trend towards a European state as 'European'. Curiously, they believe that they are good Europeans and call out all those who criticize the centralization of power and defend the idea of a Europe of freedom and diversity. Do you see the game being played here? The *true* Eurosceptics, Europe's enemies, or even Europe's traitors, are those who turn away from the idea of a politically fragmented Europe of diversity and freedom and commit themselves to the Asian draft of giant, centralistic states. The EU is not European in its current ideology.

This was also the view of the national Economist Wilhelm Röpke (18991966), an innovator of the social market economy, who pointed out that *"it is the essence of Europe to be a unity in diversity, which is why everything centralized is a betrayal and violation of Europe, even in the economic sphere."* The more than 17 million British citizens who voted for Brexit have done more for the true European idea than the EU politicians want to see. These British are the real Europeans. They want more Europe. They voted against an EU which, through its centralization, harmonization and the elimination of political competition, is the opposite of what Europe is and has made up of in the past.

Brexit gives hope. It's *more* than sand in the gears of Eurocrats' plans. It creates a precedent. It shows that the one-way road to the United States of Europe suggested by politicians is no more than a dream. It's different. Centralization and unification are not irreversible.

Since June 23rd, 2016, we know that anyone who disagrees with the planned superstate in Brussels, with all its regulations, rules and its egalitarianism, will still have the Exit-Option. Now that everyone knows that things are happening differently, further attempts at centralization can be sanctioned and slowed down. Conscious of this, Angela Merkel warned of the increasingly inspired centrifugal forces in the EU right after the Brexit vote. These forces could also strengthen the movements that are working to achieve new states in Catalonia, Scotland or northern Italy.

Whenever Eurocrats pounce on negotiations regarding a larger state, tax harmonization and more power for Brussels, non-compliant states can point out that they could hold a referendum on EU residency in the same way as in the UK. The dissenters don't even need to explicitly threaten with a referendum. Since Brexit, this option has been out in the open. It works; it disciplines. The momentum may turn away from centralization, unification, and towards freedom and competition of diverse, small and numerous political entities. In short: *more* Europe.

Why Brexit is good for Europe and what opportunities it offers are themes we want to examine in more detail below. The focus will be on why small political units are preferable to large states.

# WHY LARGE STATES ARE MORE UNSTABLE AND SMALL STATES ARE MORE HUMAN

*Once a society has become large enough to satisfy the social, economic, political and cultural needs of people, that is, when it gives them leisure to think, locations in which to debate, churches for prayer, universities for teaching, theater for inspiration, art in which to rejoice, then further growth can no longer serve its original purpose.*

*Leopold Kohr*

# THE EU AS A "CONNECTIVE SECRET WEAPON"

On December 12th, 2012, the European Union was awarded the Nobel Peace Prize in Oslo: for its commitment to peace, reconciliation, democracy and Human Rights in Europe. Representing the federation of states, the EU grandees Jean-Claude Juncker, Herman Van Rompuy and Martin Schulz received the award, which, before them, had already been received by men like Henry Kissinger, Yasser Arafat and Barack Obama.

Van Rompuy, who served as EU Council President at that time, knew to use the impact of the Euro crisis on EU policy in his acceptance speech:

> *When prosperity and employment, the foundations of our society, seem threatened, it is natural for hearts to narrow, egoism to increase and even long-forgotten judgements and prejudices to reemerge. Some, then, doubt not only joint decisions, but also the fact that joint decisions are made.*

With a look back on the history of Europe, he declared:

> *War is as old as Europe. Our continent bears the scars of spears and swords, cannons and guns, trenches and tanks.*

With reference to Willy Brandt's genuflection in Warsaw or the moment when François Mitterrand and Helmut Kohl reached out in Verdun, Van Rompuy said symbolic gestures alone could not consolidate peace. But the citizens in Europe can be reassured that there will be no new war, as...

This is where the European Union's 'secret weapon' comes into play: a unique way of linking our interests so closely together that a war becomes almost impossible. Through constant negotiation on more and more topics among more and more countries, according to the golden rule of Jean

Monnet: "Mieux vaut se disputer autour d'une table que sur un champ de bataille." ("It is better to argue at the negotiating table than on the battlefield.")

If I had to explain it to Alfred Nobel, I would say not just a peace Congress, but a perpetual peace Congress!

Admittedly, some aspects can be puzzling, and not only to outsiders.

Ministers from landlocked countries passionately discussing fishing quotas. Europarlementarians from Scandinavia debating the price of olive oil.

The European Union has perfected the art of compromise. It's not about victory or defeat, but about the fact that all countries emerge from the talks as winners.

The EU's great merit in having peace in Europe for decades is one of two deadlock arguments that are always held against EU critics. The other is globalization. A nation on its own can never meet the influx of demands that arises within it in this context. But one can only really wonder that the people in Switzerland, Liechtenstein or San Marino have not yet been completely impoverished and their countries have not yet been devastated by constant wars. By the way, it should be noted here that the small state of San Marino has no debt. And states such as Switzerland or Liechtenstein were completely neutral in both World Wars.

# LOOKING AT EVERYTHING
# FROM BOTTOM TO TOP

Let us examine the "secret weapon" of the EU, which Van Rompuy was so enthusiastic about and by means of which the interests of the EU's citizens can be connected so closely, something to bring them even closer. Let's see if it's really so ingenious, or perhaps a false argument to justify the pursuit of political size and centralization.

Of course, it's true: people have different interests. While one individual enjoys spending their holiday by the sea, the other prefers to go hiking in the mountains. Mr. A regularly cycles to work, while Mr. B has the great pleasure of driving to the office with a Porsche. The fashion taste of a woman from Rome is also likely to be different from that of a farmer in Lower Bavaria.

Beyond their basic needs, the more diverse their cultures are, the more people's interests differ. The philosophy of an official in Sicily will differ considerably from that of a small entrepreneur in Baden-Württemberg.

However, all people have something in common, no matter where they live, whether young or old, rich or poor: *every person negotiates.* This is the essential aspect of this book. This brings us to the point where it is fundamentally different from the many other books and articles dealing with the problems in Europe or the Euro crisis. In our analysis, we will strictly look at the problems and current political institutions and structures from the perspective of the individual.

Politicians are *not* doing this right now. When they look out of their ivory towers, they only see masses of people, or more precisely, masses of voters. They consider society as a whole, as if it were a society they are negotiating with and not people. "Europe" must react, show solidarity, move closer together, be equal to the USA or China in world of political importance. The majority of economists, directly or indirectly financed by the state, pursue this "top-down" approach and attempt to analyze and interpret the economic events and social developments they observe in their entirety.

Instead, we will take a "bottom-up" view, that is to say, a completely opposite perspective than the one usually used today. We will look from the bottom up and not from top to bottom. In order to understand the importance of this direction of view, a little theory about the functioning of human trade is essential. First of all, and it may sound very banal, but:

*people trade with one another!* The meaning of these five words is underestimated by some, feared by others. Especially for politicians, they hold an explosiveness that shouldn't be underestimated. Because behind human negotiation, there is a logic that cannot be refuted. After all, it cannot be denied that man negotiates. Anyone who wanted to say this would have a hard time arguing against it. They *negotiate*, too, and would therefore immediately become entangled in a contradiction.

The same condition applies to the actions of all human beings, always and everywhere: without exception, every human being seeks, through their actions, an improvement of their situation or well-being; every negotiation takes place out of a state of dissatisfaction. At least, a person wants to achieve something better through their actions, not something worse; otherwise they would not have sought to make the negotiation. If you reflect on your own negotiations, you will certainly confirm this statement. Human negotiation is always subjective. What one does in order to feel more comfortable is far from being desirable for the other. Increasing one's own well-being can also mean acting in such a way as to improve the situation of others; for example, being there for friends and family, volunteering or giving a donation following an earthquake disaster.

In addition, every human being uses resources to achieve his or her goals.

And because these resources, and our time on earth, are limited, each individual must make a judgment regarding their own goals. Every person has to decide which goals he or she prioritizes and which desires he or she will set out to achieve first.

The act of negotiating between each human being is therefore guided by individuals' goals and desires, by the means which they can use, and by the time available to them. The limited but unique amount of subjective knowledge and private information is of great help to the individual. The sum of this knowledge distributed decentrally to the people is enormous, and no authority, even the central government, which is best informed by countless statistics, not in Brussels and not in Berlin, can possess this knowledge or acquire it. Governments and politicians, however, always strive to know what is best for Germany or the EU—in immigration policy, saving the Euro, pension reform or infrastructure projects. Strictly speaking, they're really only know-it-alls.

Who could know your preferences and desires better than yourself? Who would know better than you about the resources available to you and your personal circumstances? When are you planning to purchase your next car? What does your family planning look like? Do you plan to purchase a property, or do you prefer to rent? As you come home after work, how you do so most comfortably? Where can you buy your favorite dinner for the cheapest price? How do you greet your loved one and get a laugh in return? Neither German Chancellor Merkel nor European Commission President Juncker can know all of this. They don't even know you. And yet they are determined to plan your life in important ways, referring to their experts. They block your options for negotiating through prohibitions and regulations, push you into pre-designed life choices through subsidies and government offers, for which they use a large part of the money they previously collected from you via taxes and fees.

# SOCIAL UNITS

The individual is naturally the smallest unit one can look at. One step further, beyond the individual, we find the family as the next largest social, even economic unit. This is still a fairly manageable size, as in most cases a family knows quite well about mutual interests and objectives. And the means available to achieve this are also likely to be pretty clear.

Beyond the family, things might get more difficult: do you know the wishes of your neighbor? Maybe you exchange a few words with them from time to time if you happen to meet, or maybe you're even friends. However, this doesn't mean that you would disclose your complete life plan, your goals and wishes, or your bank balance. You would have to be very good friends indeed.

The next unit to be considered is the municipality or city in which the individual lives. Surely there are still small regions where almost everyone knows everyone. But knowing each other doesn't mean knowing everything about others. This is not necessary, because in order for people to fulfill their goals and wishes, there are markets. Here, people meet to realize their interests as cooperatively and voluntarily as possible. Of course, the market must be understood here as any place (even in digital form) and any way in which and how goals of individuals are met. This ranges from simple shopping at the bakery to global, highly specialized division of labor in the production of technological equipment.

People voluntarily enter into such trade relations—in contrast to their relationship with the state—because they promise to achieve their goals. Two contractual or exchange partners value the goods that they offer to each other more highly than the goods they are willing to supply themselves. If the exchange or the business comes about, both leave the market as the winner. Here we see it again: the most general condition for human negotiation is namely the goal of improvement by negotiation. And the more free and unhindered markets are, and the more possible business partners there are available, the better it is for everyone involved.

# SPONTANEOUS MARKET ECONOMY WITHOUT THE EU

Institutions such as the EU, but also national governments, claim that they alone would be able to create the conditions for *markets*, and without their help, people would fall back into barbarism. The Oslo acceptance speech by Van Rompuy testifies to such a thought. In this context, markets have developed spontaneously even before ancient times. They existed long before government organizations formed, as we know them today.

In his book, *The Fatal Conceit: The Errors of Socialism*, the Economist and Nobel laureate Friedrich August von Hayek (1899-1992) writes, in the chapter "Trade is Older than the State," that:

> the more economic history one learns, the more misleading the idea is that the creation of a well-organized state would have culminated in the early development of culture. The role of the state is greatly exaggerated in historical accounts because, of course, we know so much more about what organized state activity accomplishes than what was achieved through the spontaneous coordination of individual efforts.

Markets have existed from time immemorial. The Agora in ancient Athens became the epitome of a marketplace and formed the opposition to the political center of power of the Acropolis. The Mediterranean Sea trade was also very strong in ancient times, with a high exchange of goods, without a state organizing or enabling it. The area of influence of the Hanseatic League in the Middle Ages and early modern times is another example of a spontaneously formed trading network. Especially since there were no states in the present sense of a territorial monopoly on the use of force during antiquity and in the Hanseatic League. For example, Hanse did not apply any state laws, but Low German legal *customs*.

Even today, at primary school playgrounds or play areas, it's possible to observe how markets develop when children start to exchange collectible pictures, such as small photos of soccer players in front of a World Cup. The same can be observed on the Internet when Bitcoin exchanges occur. It's simply in the nature of man to try to improve themselves by exchange. Thus, markets arise spontaneously. *Without* politicians and bureaucrats.

It's not governments that create markets. Perhaps they will create customs restrictions or price controls and then boast about such ingenious services. In doing so, they only lift trade barriers that they themselves have imposed on people at some point in the past. Strictly speaking, they only create a normal situation, namely that everyone can trade with anyone and enter into barter transactions. When there are reports in the press, such as in the summer of 2016, that trade with South Korea could be increased significantly due to a free trade agreement negotiated five years previously, the bureaucrats patted each other on the shoulders and congratulated each other.

So-called free trade agreements, such as TTIP (Transatlantic Trade and Investment Partnership) between the United States of America and Europe, or CETA (Comprehensive Economic and Trade Agreement), an economic and trade agreement between Canada and Europe, are called political breakthroughs. But why is there such secrecy about these deals being negotiated by state officials and industrial lobbyists? Is it perhaps not a question of real free trade, but of certain interest groups being able to maintain and strengthen their market position? If governments wanted genuine free trade, they would have *nothing* to do but free their citizens and businesses from existing restrictions that would prevent them from entering into voluntary agreements with each other at any time and without regard to any limits.

# INTERVENTION,

# CENTRALIZATION AND

# STABILITY

There are other important reasons why markets cannot be planned on a political drawing board and, above all, cannot be controlled. In his book *Antifragility*, the statistician and epistemologist Nassim Nicholas Taleb distinguishes between complicated and complex systems. How a laser robot is made and how it works is complicated. But in a complicated system there are no unexpected and unpredictable interactions, provided, of course, everything is constructed and assembled without errors. If you press a button, the desired reaction takes place.

Societies and economies are ultimately also shaped by people, but their orders have emerged spontaneously and they are *complex* rather than complicated. And in complex systems there are unpredictable and strong interactions. The larger social units are, the more complex they are, the more knowledge is available and the more decentralized this knowledge is scattered. The key difference between complicated and complex systems is the impact when pressing a button. In a complicated system the result is known, whereas in a complex system, it's not. In the latter system, knowledge is distributed decentrally and cannot be centralized. The more knowledge is decentralized, the more impossible central control becomes.

In an interview with *Foreign Policy* magazine in October 2012, Taleb came to the conclusion that "the European Union is a dreadful, stupid project," but also that "the most stable country in human history, and perhaps the most boring, is Switzerland."

# SMALL IS EFFICIENT AND STABLE

Taleb also argues that "we need smaller, decentralized governments. On paper, it may seem more efficient when one is big because of economies of scale, but in reality it's more efficient when one is small. ...An elephant can break a leg very quickly, while a mouse can be thrown out of the window without being damaged; size makes the makes the former fragile," Taleb continues.

If Switzerland is the mouse, then the EU, as well as France, Great Britain, Spain, Italy or Germany are the elephants. When political units tend to grow larger, their complexity also increases. All the more disturbing are political interventions, which, however, are not recognized as causes of disturbances because of their interdependencies. However, the interactions are perceived as disruptions and serve to legitimize further interventions by politicians. With weak economic growth or recessions, these reflexive interventions are called stabilizations or economic policies. That sounds good and lets the citizens assume that politicians have a theory and a plan.

The larger and more regulated systems are and the more they are geared for stability, the slower and more fragile they become. Especially in recent years, it has been quite textbook-like to observe how complex systems have been deprived of their variability by means of artificially created stability. Unfortunately, however, this can only be seen at the moment when something unexpected happens and systems fall into crisis. Then, the policy falls into crisis mode. Politicians step in front of microphones and start their statements with "we have to..." This is when the *know-it-alls come in*. This is followed by measures whose interaction, as we have seen, cannot be assessed by a complex system. A vicious circle.

Using the example of Switzerland, which Taleb called "the most robust place on the planet from an economic point of view," he comes to the conclusion that it is the "bottom-up" structured system of governance, combined with the size of the country, which allows for variability, and thereby gives rise to anti-fragility and strength.

It is therefore not surprising that the Federal Constitution of the Swiss Confederation does not include either a head of state or a head of government in the classical sense, and that the tasks of the federal president are limited to the chairmanship of the Federal Council and Representatives. Who would know the names of the most important Swiss politicians? Even for the Swiss, it's not particularly important to know who their current president is, as he doesn't interfere much in their lives. This is in contrast to the powerful in the EU or other nations. The latter mix themselves in with the people, and that's why they're known. They're all too happy to present themselves on a global scale and to meet from summit to summit in order to decide what appear to be necessary interventions to solve the problems they have caused themselves. Then the rather boring, stable-unstable-themed, never ending reports on political events come about.

The Economist and political scientist Leopold Kohr (1909-1994), winner of the Alternative Nobel prize (officially the *Right Livelihood Award*), was not a friend of large artificial formations and was intensively concerned with the optimal size of nations. Always an avowed opponent of the European Union, in 1993, long before the introduction of the Euro, he said the following in a conversation with a magazine:

*Stability wouldn't be a problem if the European bicycle had so many wheels that it would be able to balance itself. It wouldn't have to be steered from Brussels.*

A bicycle comparison that moves in a completely different direction was provided by former European Commission President Jacques Delors:
"Europe is like a bicycle. If you stop it, it'll fall over." What he wanted to say: there is no alternative to the ever-increasing centralization of power in Brussels.

In the search for the optimal size of the state, Kohr always drew the parallel to nature, where organisms end their growth when they reach an optimal size. He concluded, "it would be much easier for modern European history to conform to the laws of physics". Kohr preferred quality over quantity and so no one should be surprised that he, like Taleb, was a big fan of Switzerland.

In Switzerland, there is decentralization, not centralism, and the variability of the decentralized system ultimately creates stability. The findings of a "bottom-up" approach are wonderfully implemented in Switzerland: the federal government is weak and the base, the cantons and the municipalities within the cantons, is strong.

If you think logically, you can come to no conclusion other than: *small is beautiful.* That's exactly what Leopold Kohr's main realization was. What's more, with regard to Switzerland, he came to an assessment that should cause centralization politicians, or, the vast majority of politicians to gasp:

*The same idea could also work in the rest of Europe. Nothing would be easier than dividing Europe into small regions.*

The conditions for this are even available for Kohr:

*Unlike the attempt to build a single building, the opposite would hardly find natural resistance, since small regions already exist. In today's Europe, we find not only Germany but Bavaria and Saxony; not Britain, but Scotland and Ireland; not Spain, but Catalonia and the Basque country; not Italy, but Lombardy and Sicily. These regions have not disappeared due to their merger into a modern nation state. They preserve the appeal of their independent dialects, customs and literature.*

Germany, in particular, has retained much of its regional character and charm. The Allgäu, Harz, Rhineland, Siegerland, Emsland, Ostfriesland, Franconia, Münsterland, Schwarzwald, Mecklenburg lakes, Eichsfeld, Vorpommern, Uckermark, Anhalt, Oberlausitz and so many more landscapes have their unmistakable characteristics and unique charms.

Do these regions need the Brussels police machinery (or Berlin) to be culturally and economically successful? Are not EU centralization efforts a threat to regional peculiarities and cause their slow death? Could the regions be better on their own? We want to show in this book that, yes, they can do it alone. And become better. Much better.

Supporters of small political units, whether in Catalonia or Scotland, are often called "separatists" by central government politicians. Anyone entering "separatist" as the search term on the Internet and looking at the results in pictures will find heavily armed soldiers in combat suits. One won't find pictures of peacefully celebrating and *Sardana* dancing Catalans, nor any pictures from Bavaria, whose inhabitants, in a survey conducted in 2011 by the Hanns-Seidel-Foundation, expressed that almost one quarter wanted an autonomous Bavarian state.

But what is the worst thing to discover when a population group strives for independence by peaceful means? As early as 1927, the economist Ludwig von Mises (1881-1973) wrote in his work *Liberalism* about how important it is that people have a right of self-determination:

*The right to self-determination in relation to the question of belonging to the state thus means: If the inhabitants of an area, be it a single village, an area or a series of contiguous areas, have revealed by unaffected voting that they are not of the mind to wish to remain in that state to which they belong at the moment, but wish to form an independent state or wish to belong to another state, this wish must be taken into account. Only this alone can effectively prevent civil wars, revolutions and wars between states. [...]*

*However, the right of self-determination, which we are talking about, is not the right of self-determination of the nations, but the right of selfdetermination of the inhabitants of each area which is large enough to form an independent administrative district. If it were possible to grant every single person this right of self-determination, it would have to happen.*

The Principality of Liechtenstein has the only constitution in the world that provides for the right of individual municipalities to secession. It is sufficient for a separation to be decided by the majority of parishioners.

But Liechtenstein is an exception. The otherwise standard political message conveyed by politics is propaganda: *big is good and small is bad and too weak in a globalized world. There is no alternative to growing together into larger political entities, and ultimately into a world state. And that's good.*

This is the picture that is drawn, and anyone who wants to come out of a union like the EU is acting *un*-European and is old-fashioned. The associations that arise in terms such as separatism or secession cannot be negative enough.

The "secret weapon" of the EU is no more than a fake argument: its ammunition is not compromise, but propaganda, and the ultimate goal is certainly *not* the linkage of people's interests, but power struggles, elimination of competition and egalitarianism.

If one wanted to serve the people, one would only have to let them *negotiate* together in peace and for their mutual benefit. Then their interests would be served—*without* a secret weapon. Only the people themselves know their own goals and the means at their disposal.

# HOW BUREAUCRACY GROWS IN LARGE STATES

*It is in the nature of the system of state economic control to strive for utmost centralization.*

*Ludwig von Mises*

# WASTEFULNESS IN LARGE AMOUNTS

In the previous chapter we explained that size makes for fragility and, in contrast, *decentralization* creates stability. But decentralization has further positive effects. For example, it enables close contact with citizens, who might be completely lost in administrative structures that have grown above a certain size. Large structures merely create the Illusion that decisions are made conscientiously and rationally. But shiny facades with waving flags just pretend to be professional. Reality normally looks different.

Each state bureaucracy is characterized by two attributes: it looks after the money of strangers and tends to be less responsible with it than if the money were its own. Moreover, a bureaucracy does not act under competitive conditions, because there is no market for state services. If both points in themselves are a big problem, they only become more troublesome with the size of an administrative unit.

The further away a bureaucrat removes themselves from the citizen, the more difficult it becomes to hold them responsible in the event of wastefulness. Even a guilty conscience will be less associated with the latter; the less one doesn't have to look the taxpayer in the eye and admit to having squandered their money, the less one should feel the need to worry.

Would you like an example? Gladly. In the German newspaper *Handelsblatt online* on Sept. 23rd, 2016:

> *Weeds grow wild between huge cranes. A shipwreck rusts on a container dock. For far and wide there are no people, no vehicles and especially no ships to be seen. This is what seaports built with European taxpayers' money look like. A total of 42 ports in five countries (Germany, Italy, Poland, Spain and Sweden) have been audited by the*

*European Court of Auditors. The bottom-down result: the EU Commission uses taxpayers' money to promote ports that no one needs. A total of around 400 million Euros from the EU structural funds had been spent "inefficiently" by the Brussels authorities. This is a third of the total funding of 1.4 billion Euros allocated to these 42 ports, according to a report on "Maritime Transport in the EU" submitted by the EU Court of Auditors on Friday. The court of Auditors has already pointed out the problem for the second time. Six years ago, the Luxembourg Auditors complained about the nonsensical subsidization of five seaports in a first report. They wanted nothing to do with it.*

In fact, the potential for wastage increases *disproportionately* with social size. The individual controls their own expenses. They have to deal responsibly with their resources; otherwise they fall on their face. Even in the family, spending can be controlled fairly well and rational decisions can be made. *Should we pave the garden path or buy a new sofa for the living room?* The resources available, and the costs, the benefits and the preferences of those affected are very manageable in the family. This allows for a responsible decision. Even at the level of a community of homeowners, this decision-making still works.

It is already more difficult at the level of a village or city. Should a country road be repaired or rather the public swimming pool? The mayor, even if he or she has the best intentions, faces an information problem. What are citizens' wishes and preferences? What would they do with the tax money if it hadn't been taken from them? Would they rather opt for the refurbished public pool or the bump-free road? Or for something completely different?

If a reasonably satisfactory decision in the village still succeeds, the problem of information at a national level becomes immeasurable. Finally, at the EU level, the idea of a rational decision is almost grotesque. In which projects should EU subsidies flow to become useful? Where is the money best invested? There are countless possibilities. There are no limits to creativity. What are the preferences of EU citizens? What would you have done with the money, if it hadn't been taxed away? The EU Commission, or whoever ultimately decides, cannot possibly have access to all this information. In the end, as *Die Welt* reported in February 2013, money flows into nonsense projects such as a 240-meter-long ski slope in Denmark or, as just seen, in ports that are not controlled by ships.

One way forward is to act blindly without the necessary information. Another way is to boast about it and to consider this distance from the affected people as a "secret weapon". We remember. Herman Van Rompuy gushing about "Ministers from landlocked countries passionately discussing fishing-quota. Europarlementarians from Scandinavia debating the price of olive oil." There are no words.

So, the argument goes nowhere; huge political units such as the nation states, the EU or even a world government would be needed to cope with the challenges of a globalized and increasingly complex world. Indeed, the world has become more complex and with it, the information problem facing politicians and bureaucrats is even more overwhelming. But globalization doesn't make central planning and large political units like the EU more desirable or more necessary. Quite the contrary: the growing complexity increases the knowledge problem immensely, before the central decision makers carry out their decisions. The logical conclusion: the challenges of globalization make *smaller*, not larger political units necessary.

# CONTROL AND RESPONSIBILITY

The removal of decision-making from the people affected by these decisions also makes effective control difficult. If the individual wastes their money, they must live with the consequences themselves. If the family finds that they would rather have bought the sofa instead of paving the garden path, then they can only be annoyed at themselves. The mayor, who decides to have the street repaired, although the majority of citizens would have preferred to enjoy a renovated public pool, is likely to punished at the ballot box in the next municipal elections. Citizens know who to turn to in the event of waste. They know the person responsible, in smaller places, often even personally.

But who would get on the train to Brussels, to speak to an EU bureaucrat about waste or a bad investment? Which bureaucrats, anyway? There are so many. And where exactly, in the foreclosed EU complex, would one go? Those responsible are not accessible. And when it comes to the standard of living in Brussels—4,365 EU officials alone earn more than the German Chancellor—one must admit that the phrase "birds of a feather flock together" is appropriate here.

This makes control almost impossible at the EU level. EU citizens don't even know the different alternatives. Most have heard neither of the Sicilian port of Augusta nor the ski slope on the Danish Baltic island of Bornholm. It's not even possible to objectively say which project is better now, because the information is not available—yes—not available at all, as people's preferences and desires are only accessible to themselves.

The same is true of responsibility. If the individual and the family are still responsible for their decisions and have to bear the consequences themselves, it becomes more lackadaisical at the community level. The mayor can't be completely sure, what the citizens really want. And without this necessary information, they tend to act irresponsibly. The larger the political units are, the more the irresponsibility weighs down on the individual. The EU decision-maker inevitably acts irresponsibly because they don't know the costs of their actions; a wrong decision does not affect them, but the citizens of the EU.

Now the question arises: how can these problems, for example, the port project or the ski project, be solved in the face of information problems?

On the one hand, a great deal of help would be given to citizens, and the problem of information would be less serious if this decision were taken at regional or even local level. On the other hand, the market process, as Hayek called it, offers *methods of discovery* to make rational decisions. In the market, entrepreneurs compete with each other to meet the needs of their fellow human beings better and more efficiently than their rivals. To ensure this, one needs to use resources sparingly and combine them into a product that people particularly like.

If an entrepreneur uses resources to build a ski slope in Denmark, the market will reveal whether he has acted in the interest of consumers or not. If the entrepreneur makes a profit, then he has sensibly used the scarce resources of society and combined them in such a way that these resources put together as a ski slope are more valuable than as individual parts in the market. They have created an added value by purchasing resources cheaply and putting together something, in the eyes of consumers, that is more valuable. If, on the other hand, the entrepreneur suffers a loss, then the cost of the resources exceeds the product value. They have *not* been able to combine labor, natural resources and precursors into something more valuable. If the entrepreneur fails to move quickly, they will disappear from the market. The losses mean that these resources should have been used better in other ways.

Only a dynamic market process and competition allow us to solve the problem of information, to act responsibly and thus to satisfy the needs and preferences of people as well as possible. For failures and wastefulness are punished by losses, but good decisions are rewarded by profits.

This market discovery mechanism is overridden when it comes to political operation. Failures are not punished by losses. So, it's not surprising that *both* projects mentioned above were realized thanks to EU funding. The port of Sicily is practically broken down and the ski slope on Bornholm, despite the massive use of snow cannons, is used for just a few days during the year. What the EU taxpayers would have done with the money had it not been taken for the realization of these projects is written in the stars.

# CORRUPTION AND REDISTRIBUTION

Let's go back to the size of social units. Size not only increases wiggle room and shrinks responsibility for waste, it also has an impact on the honesty of individuals. Distance from this unit makes control looser, and bribery and corruption can proliferate. There is no corruption in an individual. A person wants to achieve their goals, and can also find support from their friends.

In the family, corruption is kept on a very short leash. If a female gardener is hired, who paves the garden path at a higher-than-normal price, then this is either done so intentionally, or, everything turns on its head, for example, when it comes out that the gardener is the secret mistress of the father of the family. If the mayor, based in a municipality, refurbishes the outdoor swimming pool for an inflated price by means of a friendly entrepreneur, and then invites him in return on a luxury holiday, he or she will, figuratively speaking, be tarred and feathered by the village inhabitants, which, if the village is small enough, isn't unlikely. At a national or EU level, this concept looks different. Small bribes and gratuities are made by lobbyists. Control over this is practically impossible and those responsible for projects that are too expensive and large-scale are not tangible.

Shame and scruples are typically lost in the crowd. And even if an individual never cheated on their wife with the neighbor, or received benefits at their expense, finding a solution is easier on the individual scale than with millions of unknown EU citizens. Especially if one is only a small part of the huge EU machinery. Of the 751 members of the European Parliament, only very few are known by citizens by name. Conversely, this idea applies even more: the 751 members of the European Parliament will know only a tiny fraction of the 500 million EU citizens by name.

How do you expect Jon Doe to get excited about MEPs' benefits or luxury holidays if he doesn't know the MEPs or any information about their holidays? In the masses, the bureaucrat can hide. The same applies to the almost 33,000 employees of the EU Commission. In the masses, responsibility is lost; everyone can pass it on to someone else; they can push the blame on another – and in the end, responsibility reaches no one. No one is responsible. It's true that something has gone wrong somewhere, but *where* it exactly happened and *who* bears the responsibility remains unclear. Thus, the "Brussels" machine spreads its protective coat of greatness over the actions of individual EU politicians. It may not be surprising that there's so much waste and corruption.

It's even worth having an anti-fraud and anti-corruption office in Brussels. It's a pity that the EU isn't listed on Transparency International's (2016) Country Corruption Perception Index. With Switzerland in fifth place, Singapore in seventh place or New Zealand in first place in 2014, the EU would certainly not be able to compete. Interestingly, in terms of the number of inhabitants, only small nations are found at the top ten: except for Canada at rank 9 and the Netherlands at rank 8, these are countries with a population of less than 10 million. One can see Germany at least in 10th place, but one has to look further down on the table in search of other EU countries: France only occupies rank 23, Spain is in 41st place and Italy and Greece are ranked 60th and 69th respectively.

Size also increases the scope for subsidies and redistribution, which usually fail and become unclear. In the family, redistribution is voluntary, immediately recognizable and wanted. It is also manageable in the municipality. Should wine cultivation be subsidized to make the village more attractive and draw in more tourists? Hotel owners, innkeepers and retailers are likely to benefit. But tourists also bring restlessness, noise and pollution. Advantages and disadvantages remain in view. The subsidy must pay all villagers, and yet it is distributed to an introspective number of heads. In the village of 2,000, the 1,000,000-Euro subsidy for the construction of a vineyard costs 500 Euro per person. With a family of four, that's 2,000 Euros. Resistance should be expected from those who don't hope to benefit so much from tourism.

It looks different for larger social structures, and especially for huge subsidy machinery such as the EU. There, the 1,000,000 Euro subsidy can be distributed over many more heads. Many citizens won't know about the subsidy, or notice anything related to it. Even if an EU-wide wine-growing subsidy is distributed at a total cost of €1 billion, 500 million EU citizens will face a cost of €2 per head. And for 2 Euros, hardly anyone is expected to run to the streets and protest. If, however, someone comes up with the daring idea of abolishing a wine subsidy that has already been introduced, one can be sure that the winemakers, with their tractors, will block the highways and shut down traffic to fight for their lucrative subsidy. The incentive for lobbies to benefit at the expense of the silent public is therefore much greater at the EU level than at the community or regional level. Small, well-defined groups of beneficiaries, such as winemakers, can join forces and, through the EU institutions, try to enrich themselves at the expense of the passive community, which is hardly noticed because of its size. It becomes noticeable only in the sum of the *many* lobbies, which act just like the wine growers.

Bureaucrats and officials with big budgets are like fat fish for anglers. It's worth throwing the whole fishing rod away. Bureaucrats, who have a lot of money to distribute, become the fuel for lobbyists of all kinds. No wonder then, that, where there is *little* money to distribute, there are *few* lobbyists and, where there is *a lot of* money to be distributed, there are *many* lobbyists who always seek to get the most out of their clients. According to a report by the *Süddeutsche Zeitung* of May 2014, Brussels is the second largest lobbyist in the world after Washington, with 8,000 registered organizations.

Overall, with increasing social size, redistributive actions are becoming more and more complex; no one is looking, through. Some receive agricultural subsidies, others receive general subsidies, others benefit directly or indirectly from subsidized EU infrastructure projects. Billions of Euros are pushed back and forth between countries. At the same time, taxes are paid; some pay more, others less. In addition, there is a monetary redistribution through the money system, which, in the Eurozone, also redistributes *between* countries—even more so since the outbreak of the

Euro crisis. The net result is difficult to determine and much more opaque than at the community level. The resistance to the difficult-to-understand redistribution is therefore weak. And where resistance is low, there is great leeway for lobbies and bureaucrats to launch redistributive projects. Bureaucracy can even have the best intentions. It can be an angel. But even then it's not possible for it to objectively assess a supposed subsidy requirement—we remember: bureaucracy doesn't have the knowledge, because it is distributed decentrally. And this knowledge problem becomes even *more* difficult for the bureaucrat, the bigger and more complex an area is for which they have to make decisions. The complexity of a globalized world makes small political units more desirable than ever.

# THE ESSENCE OF BUREAUCRACY

Intervention and bureaucracy are like Siamese twins. The more interventions in people's lives, the greater the bureaucracy becomes that carries out, manages and monitor these interventions. A decisive feature of bureaucracy is its inherent tendency to grow.

The entrepreneur's goal is to seek profits and avoid losses. If the entrepreneur achieves profits, he or she reaches his goal. In order to do so, he has to satisfy consumers' wishes better and more cheaply than his competitors. But what are the goals and objectives of bureaucrats? They cannot maximize profits and avoid losses. This is because they don't possess their own capital, but act with the money of others, of the taxpayer. They therefore need clear rules for their actions, so-called regulations. But what is their goal within these inflexible rules? If they can't profit, what could satisfy them? Many will perhaps seek to realize their ideology as comprehensively as possible. To this end, bureaucrats tend to want to maximize their budget. It's not even necessary to look at the EU budget to figure this out. It's sufficient to take a look at the supposedly solid German budgetary policy. The budget knows only one way: up. Since 1969, federal spending has grown from 42 billion Euros to 316 billion Euros in 2016. A bureaucracy can see itself as successful if it spends a lot of money. Being frugal won't help achieve its goals. On the contrary. The higher their budget, the greater their reputation, their power, and the number of supplementary bureaucrats under their leadership. And if there is still budget left over before the end of the year, it is usually squandered so as not to encourage a cut.

Have you ever heard of a bureaucracy that manages a state institution convening a press conference and proclaiming: "Dear fellow citizens... After a long time of reflection, I have come to the conclusion that the cost of my institution exceeds the benefit we have for society. I therefore ask that our institute be closed immediately and that I be dismissed with all my staff."? Probably not. Perhaps we can still imagine this at a community level, if the head of the Tourist Information Office finds that the benefits of their office are too low and opts for closure. But that's probably not so conceivable either. The following press statement is much more familiar to us: "Dear fellow citizens... The merit of our institution to the population is extraordinary and irreplaceable. This year, we have done great things again. (This is followed by long series of figures with quantifiable earnings, without mentioning the costs.) ...We do our best, but we could do much more and reach greater heights if only the budget were increased. I am applying for a doubling of the budget of my institution because of our social benefits."

This bureaucratic trend, which is geared towards expansion, is based on local, regional, national and EU levels. Only effective control and limitation of bureaucracy at the lower level is much easier. At a community level, citizens can better examine the Tourism Office owner's argument. If they call for a doubling of their budget, you'll probably laugh at them. You can still weigh the costs of the office and its benefits quite well. At an EU level, the argument that the benefits of the authority must be far greater than costs, and that the budget must be increased, becomes nebulous and is practically unapproachable if citizens are aware of it at all. If the European Institute for Gender Equality calls for a budget increase because the social benefits of the Institute far outweigh the costs, the citizens will not be able to judge this objectively—nobody can. Most citizens will not even notice the budget increase, let alone have an idea of the existence of this institute. Or did you already know? Citizens are just too far removed. This is how large political units open the door to bulging bureaucracy.

Conclusion: with political size, the only decentrally solvable information problem is growing. The waste of money and resources is becoming more and more overwhelming. There is increasing scope for corruption, subsidy struggles, redistribution and lobbies. Bureaucracy rages on, becoming more and more unbridled. At the same time, control and responsibility are shrinking. In the ever growing masses, decency and order are lost. Only a return to decentralization and smallness will stop and reverse these tendencies. The future belongs to smaller and smaller political units.

# WHY MANY SMALL STATES
# PROMOTE POLITICAL COMPETITION

*We don't need a European state as the EU wants it to be. And what we need even less is world state. Rather, we need a Europe and a world made up of hundreds or thousands of small Liechtensteins and Singapores.*

*Hans-Hermann Hoppe*

# THE HYPOCRISY OF THE CARTEL OFFICE

You may have heard of the Federal Cartel Office. Even the tasks carried out by this "independent federal supreme authority" are familiar to many. The Office should, casually formulated, monitor companies so that they don't merge into cartels and become so powerful as to be able to bamboozle poor consumers with tactics like price fixing. On its website, this office officially presents itself as follows: "the Federal Cartel Office is an independent competition authority whose task is to protect competition in Germany. This protection is a central regulatory task within a market-economy economic order."

There are also national antitrust authorities and the Monopoly Commission. Competition at the EU level is, of course, the responsibility of the EU Commission. The cooperation between the national supervisory authorities is coordinated by the European Competition Network (ECN). The aim is to prevent "cross-border practices of companies to restrict competition"—everything for the benefit of citizens, of course.

By the way, antitrust fines are always paid to public budgets. This is practical, after all: in the years 2007 to 2014 alone almost 3.2 billion Euros were collected. In most cases, these are punishments for illegal price fixing. The politicians in Parliament are happy about the price of their "services" (diets) financed by compulsory levies. As now, they can spend even more money and thus win the favor of any interest groups.

Competition, as an exception, must be fully accepted by the authorities, and is absolutely essential for a market-economy economic order. As always, however, those responsible act very skillfully. With terms such as "cartel" and "monopoly", citizens associate them with rather negative ideas, thinking about overpriced products and companies that abuse their market position. How nice—so the citizens should think—that there are antitrust authorities.

However, if there were truly free, unimpeded markets, there would be no consumer-damaging monopolies or cartels. Why? If a company really succeeds in producing such a good product at such an unbeatable price that its rivals have no chance, it would be because the company has better satisfied consumer demands than anyone else. If a company succeeds in achieving a strong market position, it should be distinguished rather than punished. This is because it has offered first-class products at first-class prices. At least consumers see it like this. Otherwise, they wouldn't run to the company in droves. Moreover, if a company in a free and unhindered market really is so much better than its competitors that it remains on the market alone, it will only continue to do so long as it doesn't abuse its market position, and offers its customers great products at acceptable prices. Otherwise, it's just a matter of time until another company takes advantage of the opportunity to enter the same market.

At the beginning of the internet era, the US company AOL had a position that was considered by critics to be dominant. Especially after its merger with Time Warner, many feared that the newly created company could dominate the market. But competing companies managed to stand up to the giant and presented better and cheaper options than the competitor. Who's still talking about AOL today? In the end, the business combination turned out to be one of the largest merger flops in history.

However, history also provides many examples where monopolies have produced only inferior products or a lack of diversity, but have been able to exist for a long time. Interestingly, these were/are all state monopolies. To understand this, one doesn't even have to something as radical as take a ride in a laughably inadequate Trabant, a terrible car produced by the German Democratic Republic state enterprises. Just compare the opening hours of your municipality or city with those of the supermarket where you shop regularly.

*Every coercive monopoly is the opposite of competition, and is, without exception, bad for the consumer.* This sentence would probably be supported by everyone, even the heads of the antitrust authorities, whether in Germany or in Brussels. At the same time, however, the state within its borders is, among other areas, a *compulsory* monopolist of legislation, jurisdiction, tax collection and money production. In addition, the state grants preferential treatment to certain cartels, such as the trade unions, which can so enforce minimum labor prices, by means of appropriate legislation. For example, it's forbidden for a company to dismiss a striking employee and replace it with an unemployed but willing competitor. How can this be reconciled with its claim to protect competition?

Already, when looking at the state monopoly of money (which we will discuss it in a separate chapter) the impression arises that the state only allows competition where it suits it, benefits it and doesn't oppose its own power interests.

# TAXES AND COMPETITION

We now want to examine the influence "competition" exerts on the state monopoly to be able to levy taxes. If one considers taxes as a necessary evil, then, at first, some may be relieved by this monopoly. This is because, in this case, there aren't several institutions in a national territory that demand taxes; there isn't a "mafioso" on every corner that squeezes the people out of a large part of their hard-earned income.

Unfortunately, the antitrust authorities and monopoly commissions don't take care of competition on the subject of "taxes". They leave it to governments. They *don't* care about competition, but do everything they can to prevent and curb tax competition.

If politicians really wanted to be honest, as the advertising slogans of political parties promise, then we would recommend supplementing the text we just mentioned that can be found on the Federal Cartel Office's website with the following: "The protection of competition in the area of monetary affairs, taxes, education, wage formation and all other areas where competition would harm the interests of the state, government and politics is excluded." That would be *honest* politics!

"Tax harmonization" has become a fashionable phrase. Of course, this sounds better than "control cartel". While "tax harmonization" emphasizes *solving cross-border tax problems*, as it's called, it's clear that any tax competition between EU countries should be eliminated.

As a mantra repeated a thousand times, politicians, both nationally and internationally and across all parties, demand more tax justice, the closing of so-called tax loopholes and the drainage of tax havens. Tax evasion processes are regularly used as display processes. There is always talk of tax standards. And, of course, the word "social" must also be used, and it is particularly often put it in front of the word "justice".

For example, at meetings such as those with the Finance Ministers and Central Bank Governors of the G20 in July 2016, the Chairman of the OECD, José Ángel Gurría, announced that the impact of taxes would generally have to take better account of the well-being of all people and therefore be more socially equitable: "We must reconcile tax policies that promote growth and productivity with social justice."

At the same time, citizens are fooled into thinking that state services mainly pay "the rich." And who are "the rich"? They are always "the others."

However, this can be a miscalculation. The state's achievements don't fall like Manna from heaven. Whenever there is more investment in public education, health, transport and safety, it's said that the rich should be asked to pay. That it's always "the others" that pay, so state benefits cost the rest nothing; this is, so to speak, the great lie of the welfare state. This lie is convenient. For it also includes attempts by the "evil richies" to fight back, by means of tax evasion and the use of tax loopholes. So, the politicians find other fields of action. They must prevent the rich from eluding paying the bill for the welfare state. A deception, because ultimately, the citizens pay the bill themselves. But at least this noble political task can satisfy our feelings of envy, right? And how nice it is that people can so easily play against each other? The game "robbing Peter to pay Paul" continues cheerfully on.

It is not surprising that low-tax countries are increasingly becoming the target of campaigns launched by higher-tax countries. Of course, tax havens are thorns in the sides of politicians who tax their citizens to hell. Many readers will remember when, in 2009, the then Federal Minister of Finance Peer Steinbrück found satisfaction in Switzerland's actions, after they had bowed to pressure, to loosen their tax secrecy in the suspected case of tax evasion: "The cavalry in Fort Yuma doesn't always have to ride it out; sometimes it's enough for the Indians to know that they're there." Steinbrück, at that time the highest tax collector in Germany, had, on the sidelines of a G20 Finance Ministers meeting, threatened that Switzerland would otherwise end up on the black list of tax havens. Even using thieves that offer stolen bank data on CDs, Big Brother is doing its business. The end justifies all means. Why is there not a blacklist of tax shelters?

Because the vast majority of the country has fallen into the fairy tale that the rich pay for the welfare state; this means the government doesn't have to expect resistance to this kind of politics. Even the idea that tax competition could be beneficial is alien to many, and to most of them this idea will even appear disgusting. How else should the state finance itself? Finally, tax revenues enable it to fulfil its duties as a sovereign. At this point, it's almost taboo to discuss the idea that seemingly sovereign tasks of the state could also be resolved privately. This would go beyond the scope of this book. However, in a brief digression, let us turn to the fact that taxes affect the creation of wealth in an economy. And we don't mean the obvious consequence of taxes that make work and production less attractive. Or would you suddenly want to work more if you only received 40 euros instead of 50 Euros net the hour because of higher taxes? When the rate of return for our work decreases, it becomes cheaper for us to have free time at the same time. So, we will tend to work less and enjoy more free time. The same applies to production.

From this insight, we conclude that it's beneficial to the prosperity of the people to keep the tax burden as low as possible. Thus, the performance of an economy can be maintained and increased. In other words, the price of government services should be as low as possible. That this can only be achieved through competition, i.e. *tax* competition, should be clear.

# DIGRESSION

*Life is short. People are impatient and want to achieve their goals sooner rather than later. But because people have different preferences, they differ in their degree of impatience. It follows that people have a different time preference. If someone is more consumer-oriented and rather unwilling to save, one speaks of a tendentially higher time preference. The more future* goods are required in the absence of immediately available goods, the higher the time preference. If, for example, Person A is only prepared to waive the immediate receipt of 100 Euros if they are promised 110 Euros in a year, they have a higher time preference than Person B, who renounces the immediate receipt of 100 Euros for the receipt of 102 Euros in a year. The time preference of individuals will change in the course of their lives and is also determined by external influences.

The collection of taxes can have a decisive influence on time preference. If taxes for savers are increased, the net return on the capital invested by them will be reduced. But if the yield on savings decreases, it becomes cheaper to consume more. One will probably save less and consume more. Thus, the time preference tends to increase.

If the state continues to pay tax to a third party as a transfer payment, their leisure time becomes cheaper because they now have to work less than before, or no longer at all, for the same money. This third party will also tend to save less, because they can rely on state social benefits. Thus, their time preference also increases.

However, when, in a society, everyone's time preference increases through taxation and redistribution, one tends to save less and consume more. And if less is saved and more is consumed, less money is available for new investments or replacement investments. Consequently, productivity cannot be increased to the extent that would have been the case without the tax increase. Productivity may even decrease. Society becomes poorer than it would have been without the tax increase.

# CLOSED BORDERS FACILITATE
# THE "EXIT"

But how can tax competition be achieved? Admittedly, it works a little differently and more indirectly than in competition in the private sector. If the buns aren't crispy enough at the "Crackle" bakery, one can always visit the "Crinkle" bakery 100 meters further on. Private sector products are about getting the best product as cheaply as possible. We change our supplier to get a crispy bun.

Taxes, on the other hand, are not a good thing to gain, but an evil that needs to be avoided, or at least minimized. To escape a high-tax country is a little more complicated than to change bakeries. In practice, it means permanently relocating one's place of residence. This involves measures such as: finding a new job or relocating a company's main office, resolving the household, looking for a new home, organizing a change in schools for the children. And these aren't the only things that need to be done if you decide to move your future center of life somewhere else.

As a rule, you will find yourself living with a different language or in a different culture. It's particularly difficult if the country you want to leave is very large. It's precisely these two arguments that will discourage many from taking the final step. Whoever has to leave relatives and friends behind and make mutual visits halfway around the world will think twice before finally biting into the sour apple, staying where they are and grudgingly settling their unfair tax bill.

As the size of the state increases (and here we mean its territorial expansion) the number of obstacles that prevent a citizen from moving his or her central life grows. From this point of view, too, the increasingly demanding, intensified concept of European integration receives a more than bland connotation. Integration means, above all, harmonization of tax rates for Euro rates—to the highest possible level. In order to limit tax competition, the EU tax cartel, which seems to be driving its mischief beyond the radar screens of the cartel offices, has proposed a minimum VAT rate of 15 per cent. In other words, the member states have committed themselves not to lower this tax below 15 percent. So, there are supranational tax agreements already. The United States of Europe would certainly turn the citizens of Europe into a self-service shop for politicians and bureaucrats by eliminating tax competition.

That's why small political units are indispensable for a functioning tax competition. If the taxes in Country A are too high, or if one thinks they can't get adequate compensation for their taxes, such as top-notch, traffic jam-free roads or an excellent education system for their children, the decision to move to Country B will be a lot easier, to the point where the roads and the schools, because of the state, will not be much better, but at least the taxes will be bearable. Everyone understands this; with this one argument it should be made clear that a deeper European Integration will not serve the interests of the citizens, but would prevent tax competition because this concept threatens the state's tax money bag.

For the taxpayer it's easier to move to a smaller state. In an environment of small states, Jon Doe Taxpayer can do the same thing, which today, almost only the so-called super-rich can afford. And then, there comes the Exit. It makes a difference, if you can leave a state behind after 10 miles instead of 1,000 miles. If the same language is spoken at the desired destination and you don't have to leave your normal cultural space, it's much easier to set up your tent than where you're squeezed like a lemon in order to increase government revenues. You don't have to give up all your friends and relatives and you can visit each other regularly without much effort.

Conversely, from the point of view of a state, with a proximity of borders, the pressure to keep the taxpayers productive in the country increases. This also applies to companies. Everything we have said so far about the possible migration of people is of course equally true for companies, which are often easier to migrate.

If a state faces the withdrawal of the tax cows it has milked, it ultimately has two options. Either it has to close the borders and build a wall like the GDR or impose a massive tax on individuals that want to move away. Or, governments and politicians have to make an effort to offer people and businesses a good value for money, comparable to a holiday region that's competing with other regions for holiday guests. Similar to advertising for hotel guests, a government has to try, with attractive conditions, to bring the smartest minds into the country. And they may come directly from the neighborhood, as, over there, they're getting harassed with high taxes and proliferating bureaucracy, forcing them to co-finance an over-abundant supply state.

For example, in an independent Savoie, now a French Département, members of government could seek to focus on protecting their own citizens' lives, freedom and property, but not to interfere in their lives. And that at a very low "price", i.e. at a minimum tax rate. Many residents (and also companies) of the neighbouring Isère Départment might find this so attractive that they would relocate to Savoie. They wouldn't even have to learn another language. And their friends and relatives could visit at any time without much effort. In the neighboring Isère, tax consumers would mostly be left behind. The government there would have to think very quickly about a concept of keeping the residents and companies within the country. It would, for its part, be forced to reduce expenditure and tax rates and, more generally, to allow more freedom. This is because it wouldn't be able to last too long with naught but consumption and no production. This example can be applied to any other region: Bavaria and Austrian Tyrol, Spain and Catalonia, Saxony and Schleswig-Holstein. Perhaps this would even put an end to the ongoing dispute in Belgium between Fleming and Walloonia.

Once again, we recognize that large political and economic units are detrimental to the well-being of society, because they hinder effective tax competition. The larger the territory, the more difficult it is for the taxpayer to protect himself from the state's access to income and wealth. For the latter, a world state would become the Super-Gau. Then, the total tax monopoly would be complete. To escape taxes would be possible only for those who transferred their residence to another planet. But even there, politicians have already marked their territory by flags – as Neil Armstrong once impressively demonstrated on the moon.

Tax policy has long ceased to be just a means to an end. That is, to use tax revenues to cover the costs of maintaining a state order, namely a legal system with the protection of citizens and their property. Instead, tax policy has become a redistributive instrument. Taking from one to give to the other is the political motto. This creates dependents, whose votes can be as certain as politicians in the next elections. And with the redistributive politicians and bureaucrats themselves, there's always something left hanging.

This was completely clear to Ludwig von Mises when he wrote in his work, *Human Action*:

*Tax should become a tool of deliberate intervention in the transmission of the market economy. Tax policy was designed as a means of interventionist economic policy; it was not at all intended to create taxation as neutral as possible; it was precisely intended as a means of "active" social policy.*

# POLITICIANS DON'T PAY TAXES

Politicians will *always* find reasons for increasing taxes or harmonizing tax rates to prevent competition. Then, again, the phrase-like sentences that usually begin with "we must" come forward, like the post on July 23rd, 2016 in the *Frankfurter Allgemeine Zeitung,* in which two leading SPD politicians demanded a wealth tax:

> *We must invest in the future: in good education, efficient transport, safety and social cohesion. All this without new debts and with a relief for the middle income. Sounds like trying to square a circle? But it's not. In Germany, wealth is growing, while inequality is also growing. In order to activate funds for urgently needed investments, two clear announcements are needed. First, stop tax fraud that cuts billions away from our common good. Secondly, mega-incomes and mega-assets must adequately contribute to the financing of what their wealth is based on. A vast majority shares this view. [...] Taxes are never an end in itself. We are talking about more investment in infrastructure, education or access to information, that is, more justice.*

This quote provides exemplary proof of *how* politics works. There are the typical terms that can be used to create good sentiment: *social cohesion, growing inequality, tax fraud, the common good, mega-wealth, more investment, more justice... An overwhelming majority share this view.* Of course! Who doesn't want more infrastructure, education or access to information if the rich pay for it all? There is nothing more to add to the great lie that's already been mentioned. Although, perhaps, such demands are usually those of politicians, i.e. a group of companies that isn't productive (often even *before* their political career) that doesn't pay net tax. "How? No taxes?" Many will now object; politicians will even protest, refer to their payroll and the wage tax deduction reported within. However, the explanation is quite simple: politicians in government, parliaments, civil servants and public employees are all *tax beneficiaries*. Their salaries are financed by tax. Do we need to go through the thought experiment? Where would the politicians' net income be if there were no taxes? Right, at zero. The individual whose income comes from tax money is a *net tax consumer*. And, bottom line, whoever is a net tax consumer pays no taxes.

As tax consumers, therefore, politicians always strive for higher tax revenues out of self-interest. There are an abundance of these people in the population, in the form of those who also pay net taxes, who are unproductive and live on taxes. Together, they go on the hunt for additional tax revenue. When hunting for taxes, however, insatiability rules. Tax competition is only in the way of quitting this insatiability and must be eliminated.

If you still have doubts regarding this greed for ever higher tax revenues, the following figures may help you make the leap. In 1991, the first year after the unification of the two German states, the tax revenues of the federal government, federal states and municipalities in Germany were still at 338 billion Euros; 673 billion Euros were collected in 2015—an increase of quite exactly 100 percent. The money was still not enough. Would you like another example? Anyone who earns 1.3 times the average wage today, i.e. around 53,000 euros, pays the peak tax rate in Germany. Six decades ago, this was 17 times (!) the average. Despite these breathtaking numbers, there's never enough money. Between 2000 and 2015, Germany's debt rose from about 1.2 trillion to over 2 trillion euros.

Let us recall two chapters ago, in which we looked at the "bottom-up" society from the point of view of the individual. Only the individual himself or herself knows the importance of their goals and their means at their disposal. Only they know their personal time horizon, and only they have the exclusive knowledge that no other human being has. Everyone therefore knows how best to use their income and wealth, which ultimately leads to greater prosperity and productivity in the interaction with other market participants. Every tax-euro that is taken away from the citizens stops them from obtaining a means of achieving their goals, and is instead used by politicians who can't even know these goals.

Together, with the findings from our excursus, we conclude that taxes cannot be low enough. The lower, the better. Every Euro that *doesn't* end up in the hands of governments and bureaucrats, but remains with the citizens, serves to raise the prosperity of the economy. Tax competition is thus beneficial because it provides for lower taxes.

# COMPETITION FOR POLITICIANS, TOO

The benefits of competition are not limited only to taxes. The same applies to regulations or other interventions in people's lives. Small political units mean more intense competition. This is because, then, there are more units and more detailed borders. They make the Exit Option cheaper, forcing the powerful to unintentionally restrain their grip on the citizen's pocket, and make more effort to provide a higher quality environment, such as a good education system or good infrastructure.

Once again, the comparison with the small "family" unit can contribute to a better understanding. Could a father force his adult children to pay him 50 percent of their income? Could he tell them that they're not allowed to drink alcohol at home, that they have to pay for overpriced wind power, that they're only allowed to use only ridiculous energy-saving bulbs in their room, or that they have to introduce a Veggie Day? Most children would probably move out immediately. Even a mayor will barely be able to ban alcohol consumption or go through with a tax on meat consumption in the amount of 100 percent. Also, the mayor would probably be subject to a massive settlement of people from other cultures at the expense of his citizens' difficulties. The people would vote with their feet and leave the village or the district in droves. Even at the regional level, voting with feet and changing residence is realistic when it comes to attacks on citizens' property. If one looks at giant states like the former Soviet Union, it becomes clear what a state can do to its citizens if the option of "voting with one's feet" is practically excluded.

# SMALL STRUCTURES PROMOTE FREE TRADE

The situation is similar with customs duties. A family man would probably be declared crazy if he said: "We want to be self-sufficient. We will plant our own food, cut our hair ourselves, build our own means of transportation and treat ourselves in the event of illness. In order to ensure that this is reasonably adhered to, I will impose duties on all goods and services that we buy from non-family members." A family shouldn't let itself produce everything; otherwise it would be on the verge of starvation. One needs the free exchange of goods, services and capital with the rest of the world. To levy tariffs and to live self-sufficiently borders on suicide. The consequences of bad politics are immediately felt here.

In a self-contained city, one thing is similar. It needs open borders, not only because its inhabitants want or even need to travel to the rest of the world, but also in order to import all the goods that are cheaper elsewhere or that don't exist in the city. The independent city must be cosmopolitan. Only in this way can the city enjoy all the benefits of international division of labour. It's not surprising that city states such as Monaco, Andorra, San Marino or Liechtenstein don't impose duties on EU products. Giant empires such as the Soviet Union, which, albeit badly, self-produced a wide range of products and services, can tend to afford to live independently and levy customs duties. The impact of poor policies is not as immediate and visible here as in small states. It follows that the smaller the political units, the greater the pressure on free trade and open borders.

Open borders for goods, services and capital doesn't automatically mean unlimited immigration. Especially with today's social security systems, welfare migration into social dependency would open the floodgates.

The American economist and Nobel laureate Milton Friedman thought so, too (1912-2006):

*You can have a welfare state and you can have open borders. But you can't have both at the same time.*

A well thought-out immigration law is needed here. This is the only way to prevent conflicts in society. Small political units also offer huge advantages over giant states in this case. Not only will small states look very closely at who is immigrating into them, but they will also insist on qualified professionals, who raise the standard of living of the country. In addition, one could work in a micro-state environment in another country, without necessarily having to live there. They could commute to work, because the distances are small.

If small states are pursuing an unwise immigration policy, then the government must fear that their own population will take the plunge. The borders are not far away.

# COMPETITION WHEN IT COMES TO MONEY

Institutional competition is also beneficial in terms of money. The family man will hardly be able to force the family members to keep their money reserves in a currency that is constantly losing value. Members would quickly convert this currency into more stable alternatives that they can use outside the house. The same applies to city states. They, too, are hardly able to impose on their citizens a currency that loses more value than the alternatives available behind the city borders. Citizens would simply keep their savings in the currency of the neighboring city and, if necessary, buy and sell goods there. This also explains the success of the Hamburg Mark

Banco currency, which became a symbol of the solidity of the Hamburger Salesmen through its relative stability in value.

The larger the national territory and the fewer political units that exist, the more institutional competition is suspended—even in the case of money. Citizens increasingly see themselves as defenseless and without alternative Since the Euro has entered Europe, citizens of the traditional high-inflation countries on the Mediterranean Sea or even in eastern Europe no longer have the chance to keep their savings in Deutsche Mark. Before the Euro, they were able to sell their weak domestic currencies and exchange them into Deutsche Mark. This was a kind of sanction mechanism for particularly irresponsible money politicians who had to watch the value of their currency crumble. Today, the currency competition is passé. At least in the Eurozone. The competition by the Deutsche Mark was eliminated and the Bundesbank was removed. Even the Germans today lack this alternative. They, too, are trapped in the Euro.

"Good money" and a well-functioning money system are very important for an economy. To live up to the importance of "money", we have dedicated a separate chapter to this topic.

As an intermediate conclusion and generally speaking, the closer people are to the border of another country, the easier it is for them to escape conditions that do not support their well-being, such as excessive taxes or customs duties, oppressive regulations, arbitrary reprisals, mass immigration or inflationary currencies. The closer the border, the easier a change in location becomes. Thus, small economic units are a guarantee of citizens' freedom.

# INNOVATION AND COMPETITION

The competition between political units offers other advantages in addition to making an Exit easier. It makes it easier to compare and experiment. The invaluable benefits of comparing and experimenting start in small places. If your neighbor begins to use a new irrigation system for his or her garden and you're playing with the idea of also buying such a system, you may want to ask them how satisfied they are with it. If, after a few weeks, you observe a large flood in your neighbor's garden, you will probably refrain from purchasing this brand. However, if your neighbor is very enthusiastic about their purchase and the garden blooms like never before, you may consider buying a similar model, if not the same. This is how experimentation works. Someone is trying something new. We compare the old with the new, our garden with the neighbor's. What works is copied; what doesn't work is dropped. We learn. In this way, innovations are created and disseminated.

Comparing and experimenting also helps at a community level. When a municipality organizes a new Wine Festival for the first time, which proves to be a huge success, the neighboring municipalities would probably consider setting up a similar festival. What makes one region good, another can copy.

If a country has a stable currency, then it will find imitators. The Deutsche Mark was admired worldwide for its stability. Although it lost most of its purchasing power during its existence, it did so much more slowly than other currencies. Foreign states tried to do the same as the Bundesbank. The Dutch Central Bank followed the monetary policy of the Bundesbank very closely.

In addition, the comparison with the Deutsche Mark was feared by foreign politicians. In particular, the French politicians considered the D-Mark as a threat. The frequent devaluation of the Franc vis-à-vis the Deutsche Mark brought to the attention of French citizens how their currency lost value compared with their neighboring currency. And compared to the German central banks, French politicians and central bankers were doing shamefully poorly. It's no wonder that French policy was working towards the introduction of a single currency. Therefore, both competition and the unflattering comparison with the Deutsche Mark could be prevented (See Chapter 5).

Today, there is only *one* European Monetary Policy. It's no longer possible to compare different currencies within the Eurozone. The Euro has also taken away the opportunity to experiment in monetary policy. The Eurozone does not provide for individual states or regions to reintroduce the Deutsche Mark, to try out a precious metal currency or even to use Bitcoin instead of the Euro. If there were competition, solid currencies could spread and bad money would disappear from the market.

However, all is not yet centralized in the EU. There remain many opportunities for comparison between EU countries. Let us take a look at the labor market regulation. For decades, the heavily regulated labor markets in Spain seemed to be responsible for much higher structural unemployment than the very liberal labor market legislation in Denmark. Those who wanted less unemployment in their country would prefer to copy the Danish laws instead of those in Spain. Once the United States of Europe exists, which politicians want, and if labor market legislation is 'harmonized', this comparison will also disappear, at least within the EU.

The more political units there are, the more diverse the possibilities for comparison and experimentation are. For many small units, experimentation and the resultant learning process will be much more intense and dynamic. The power of innovation is exploding.

# GOETHE ALREADY KNEW

Especially for science and the arts, this kind of experimentation is of great importance. If there are many political entities, there will be strong competition to attract the best scientists and artists. To this end, universities, education systems and the cultural landscape must be attractively designed. The consequences of cultural competition can also be traced very well historically. The economist Roland Vaubel, in an essay, looked at the question of why Baroque and Renaissance music emerged in Italy and Germany and not in centralist France. Vaubel came to the conclusion that it was precisely the political fragmentation of Italy and Germany that led to this musical bloom through intense competition for the musicians. The various royal courtyards sought out the musicians and tried to win them over with attractive working conditions.

Germany's greatest poet Johann Wolfgang von Goethe (1749-1832) also drew a link between cultural bloom and political competition:

> *What makes Germany great comes from an admirable folk culture, which permeated all parts of the country evenly. But does this not come from individual princely seats—the carriers and carers of this culture? Suppose, for centuries in Germany, only the two residential cities of Vienna and Berlin existed, or even just one; I would be interested to see the outcome of German culture in this case. Yes, it's also widespread prosperity that goes hand in hand with culture! Germany has over twenty universities distributed throughout the country and over a hundred equally widespread public libraries. There is also a large number of art collections and galleries in all natural kingdoms, for every prince has taken care to bring such good and beautiful things into his environment. High schools and schools for technology and industry are in abundance. Yes, there's hardly a German village that doesn't have a school. But how did this last point play out in France?*

In Germany, not everything was concentrated in the capital of a big state like France or the eastern giant empires. The many independent political units in Germany—the words expressed by Goethe, of which there were 39—were in intense competition. Is it surprising that the time of German small states was also the time of cultural flourishing? In the 19th century the most prestigious universities in the world, in Germany, competed for the brightest minds. There, the university system was revolutionized and became a model for the whole world. Germany is experiencing a unique cultural development.

From Johann Sebastian Bach (1685-1750), Georg Friedrich Händel (16851756), Joseph Haydn (1732-1809), Wolfgang Amadeus Mozart (1756-1791), Ludwig van Beethoven (1770-1825), Franz Schubert (1797-1828), Robert (1810-1856) and Clara Schumann (1819-1896), from Richard Wagner (18131883), to Johannes Brahms (1833-1897), as well as many other German composers, contributed to the musical landscape of Europe.

With poets such as Christoph Martin Wieland (1733-1813), Johann Gottfried Herder (1744-1803), Friedrich von Schiller (1759-1805), Friedrich Hölderlin (1770-1843), Jacob (1785-1863) and Wilhelm Grimm (1786-1859), Johann Wolfgang von Goethe (1749-1832), Heinrich von Kleist (1777-1811), Franz Grillparzer (1791-1872), Heinrich Heine (1797-1856), Theodor storm (1817-1888) or Theodor Fontane (1819-1898), German literature flourished.

Philosophy was developed by thinkers such as Gottfried Wilhelm Leibniz (1646-1716), Immanuel Kant (1724-1804), Johann Gottlieb Fichte (17621814), Georg Wilhelm Hegel (1770-1831), Friedrich Schelling (1775-1854), Arthur Schopenhauer (1788-1860), Ludwig Feuerbach (1804-1872), Karl Marx (1818-1883) and Friedrich Nietzsche (1844-1900).

What's more, there was also a unique phase of creation in the scientific world, which continued until the days of the Emperor. Individuals such as Georg Christoph Lichtenberg (1742-1799), Georg Ohm (1789-1854), Carl Friedrich Gauss (1777-1859), Alexander (1769-1859) and Wilhelm von Humboldt (1767-1835), Justus von Liebig (1803-1873), Heinrich Schliemann (1822-1890), Ernst Mach (1838-1919), Heinrich Hertz (1857-1894), Otto Lilienthal (1848-1896), Robert Koch (1843-1910), Ferdinand Braun (18501918), Wilhelm Röntgen (1845-1923), Carl Benz (1844-1929), Rudolf Diesel (1858-1913), Max Planck (1858-1947) or Albrecht Einstein (1879-1955) contributed to groundbreaking findings.

Without exaggeration, it can be said that, at this time, Germany was a leader in music, literature, philosophy and science. A popular saying dates from this period: *the land of poets and thinkers.*

The "small state mentality" wasn't able to prevent the cultural and intellectual domination of Germany. On the contrary, and as Goethe correctly recognized, it was responsible for this brilliant ascent. The decentralized units competed for the best people. The numerous political units were busy inventing, trying out and experimenting with innovative educational institutions and methods, with new styles of music or literature and with scientific research. The small, independent centers and minds stimulated each other. It was a unique cultural and intellectual dynamic.

German culture continued to benefit for a long time from the fragmentation of the small German states. Even today, the aftermath of this tradition of decentralization is still noticeable. The historian Peter Watson writes in his book *The German Genius*: "Germany in January 1933, when Hitler became Chancellor was, without a doubt, the world's intellectual leader." In fact, until 1933, there were more German Nobel laureates than American and British combined. The National Socialist principals (*Gleichschaltung*) and minority persecution, especially of Jewish intellectuals, brought Germany's leadership position to an abrupt halt. However, the so profitable fragmentation had already ended with the establishment of the German Empire in 1871, when the disastrous centralization of Germany strengthened and its gradual decline began.

# OPEN STAGE FOR "PRIVATE CITIES"

Today, new hope is springing up. The resistance to centralization in the EU is increasing. Brexit is only *one* expression of this resistance. At the same time, competition is able to pave new paths. For the states could soon face new competition by the establishment of free, private cities, which could organize themselves like a profit-oriented company. Initial considerations in this direction are already being made. The co-founder and former CEO of Deutsche Rohstoff AG, Titus Gebel, is dedicated to this topic. He is convinced that everything we know about product and service markets can also be transferred to the co-existence of people. In a guest post for the *Neue Zürcher Zeitung* in June 2016, Gebel wrote:

> *The citizen would suddenly become a courted customer who could change supplier at any time, instead of constantly having to act as a cow for milking, who has to be taxed if he wants out. [ ... ] The operating body would be a service provider that has to make an effort, and can't simply change the rules to the detriment of its customers when it feels like it. Competition would ensure that there would be many different models of coexistence, something suitable for every taste. The degrees of freedom, innovation and self-responsibility would be consistently high. And if this were all too much, one would just go into an All-Inclusive-System that takes away all decisions. After one generation at the most, such private systems would be more prosperous, freer and more peaceful than anything we've come to know so far.*

If the "protection of competition is a central regulatory task in a market based economic order", as it says on the Federal Cartel Office's website, then there must be a reason why state monopolies—including the right to raise taxes—with Cartel Offices and monopoly commissions fall through the grid. The reason is obvious: while competition is beneficial to people, it is detrimental to the ruling elites.

Small, competitive, political units would generate enormous technological and cultural dynamics. Citizens could more easily sanction over-regulation, customs duties and other interference in their freedom. Political competition, as in goods markets, would increase the quality of state services, especially the protection of life, limb, freedom and property, and reduce "prices" or taxes. And who wouldn't like to pay fewer taxes?

# WHY COMPETITION IS UNDESIRABLE IN OUR MONEY SYSTEM

*To create a world with only one government, a central bank currency, the biggest and most important obstacle preventing the implementation of this idea must be destroyed – and this is gold.*

*Ferdinand Lips*

# THE ROLE OF "MONEY" IN THE ECONOMY

We have already pointed out several times in the course of this book that money plays a fundamental role in an economy. It's even *the* decisive element for politics. Monetary power makes it easier for the state to finance a sprawling bureaucracy, to set up an otherwise unviable welfare system to bribe the citizens or finance armies that are capable of more than defense. In short, the monopoly on money allows the state to become far bigger and more powerful than it would be possible *without* the power over the money. That's why the issue of *money* cannot be preserved if we consider how to limit the power and size of states.

The gold mentioned in the above quote by the Swiss banker Ferdinand Lips (1931-2005) no longer plays any role as money in today's currency structure. The following two quotations from former central banks alone show that this is not wanted.

For example, Paul Volcker, chairman of the US Federal Reserve from 1979 to 1987, once said: *Gold is the enemy.*

His successor, Alan Greenspan (until 2006), "The Market Mage", as he was called for a long time, wrote long before his time as head of the central bank an article entitled "Gold und wirtschaftliche Freiheit " (Gold and Economic Freedom), which appeared in *The Objectivist* magazine. It says:

*Without a gold standard, there is no way to protect savings from confiscation through inflation. There is no safe store of value. If that were the case, the government would have to declare its possession illegal, as it did in the case of gold. [ ... ] The fiscal policy of the welfare state demands that property owners have no opportunity to protect themselves. This is the shabby secret behind the demonization of gold by the advocates of the welfare state. Government debt is simply a mechanism for the "hidden" confiscation of wealth. Gold prevents this insidious process. It protects property rights. Once one understands this, the hostility of the welfare state supporters to the gold standard is no longer difficult to comprehend.*

Many other statements by central banks, bankers and politicians could be cited, but this alone isn't enough.

Fundamental to the following considerations is the understanding of what *money* actually is.

Money is the generally accepted means of exchange, the most marketable asset in an economy. This means the good that is best for indirect exchange; not goods against goods, but money against goods. In order to find out which commodity is most marketable, contrary to popular opinion, there is no need for government intervention. The finding of the best form of money is done without a drawn-up plan, without a planned economic determination of state political or central bank bureaucracy. This is done by market participants themselves, that is, by *people negotiating,* unaffected and without external coercion. From this point of view, precious metals, especially gold and silver, have emerged as the ultimate means of payment since time immemorial.

Of course, Alan Greenspan, already quoted, knows that. In 2014, he said in an interview:

*Gold is a currency. It is still, demonstrably, a first-class currency. No Fiat currency, including the Dollar, can match it.*

History teaches that people have chosen gold and silver as money through their negotiations over a period of several thousand years. In the sum of this negotiation there is an incredibly large amount of knowledge and experience that even the best-informed central planners can never have.

# MONEY FROM NOTHING AND

# COTTON

Unfortunately, the money that we (have to) use on a daily basis today, and precious metals, have nothing left to do with each other. If banknotes used to be certificates that pretended to be a well-defined quantity of gold or silver, banknotes today are only cotton slips claiming... nothing. You only get your purchasing power from the trust that you as a holder can still buy something for tomorrow. The same applies to money in the form of bits and bytes on our accounts.

Printing a cotton bill costs only a few cents and creating electronic money on the computer has practically no cost. For those who have the privilege of making practically free money and then shopping at will, the temptation is, of course, quite great to do just that. The situation is different with the production of precious metal money. Whether gold or silver, both metals have to be removed from the ground with a great deal of effort and laboriously processed until they are finally used in coin or ingot form. The annual gold stock grows worldwide at an annual rate of about 1.5 percent. The amount of paper and book money in circulation, on the other hand, can be expanded at *any* time at the push of a button, which also happens constantly, with growth rates, which are often at 10 percent or more per year. The countless inflations and hyperinflations in human history around the globe wave hello.

Money is something very important in a labor-sharing society. And because money is so important, in any case, it is argued that the state must take care of the monetary system. A pseudo-argument.

The truth is that governments have always been short of cash. There's never enough money. If government revenues ever exceed government spending, then that's no more than an unplanned coincidence. When answering arguments about why they always lack money, politicians are never embarrassed. First, an investment program must stimulate the economy, and sometimes, the spending on social affairs pokes a hole in the treasury. One can pass the buck onto anyone or anything. In the end, however, it is always the desire to bribe and corrupt citizens with supposed gifts in order to buy their vote. The larger the spending, the more power lies in the hands of bureaucrats and politicians and the more one can do good for friends and voters.

# THE STATE AND POWER OVER THE MONETARY SYSTEM

The most democratic source of revenue available to governments for its expenditures is taxes. These are discussed in parliament. If tax revenues are not sufficient to meet the spending requirements, politicians will take the way of least resistance. And that is, instead of increasing taxes, borrowing and creating debt. This form of financing is convenient, and citizens' opposition is very limited, as they hope to benefit from the public services that can be funded. If taxes were raised to finance a new social program, such as the integration of migrants, citizens would clearly be aware that the new program also has costs for *them.* Resistance would be inevitable. For example, very few are happy about a VAT increase. However, if the integration program is financed through the issuance of new debts, the costs remain largely hidden. If new money is printed at some point to settle the government debt created by the program, then prices start to rise (or fall less sharply than they would otherwise have done). Citizens may be paying 10 cents more at the pump than they would have done if the integration program had never started. However, few will think to connect the higher gas prices with the integration program. The resistance is therefore lower. This means that financing via debt is far more attractive to politicians than a tax increase. No wonder our federal debt is always rising to new heights.

Public debt at a large scale, as we unfortunately know today, is only possible *because money is no longer covered by trust,* neither by gold nor by real savings. Money arises from nothing, at the moment of issuing a bank loan. We live in a purely paper money system, and to grant loans, no real savings are necessary today, because the banking system is organized as a partial reserve system, and, the reserve of banks on deposits by the ECB is only held at one (!) ridiculous percent.

If we had a currency tied to gold, governments would ultimately have to levy taxes to settle their debts. Because you can't print gold. This sets a ceiling on public debt, namely the tax burden that is still sustainable or enforceable. Because governments can now print paper money (or cotton money) through their central bank, and the banking system can also make money from scratch to buy government bonds, it's possible to repay the government debt simply by producing new debt and new money. In a paper money system, the debt possibilities of governments are multiplying.

Now it becomes clear why governments have always been eager to gain control of the monetary system. Only in this way was it possible for them to design the money system according to their wishes and ideas, and to get rid of restrictive and disciplining gold. Therefore, from the beginning of the 20th century onward, the monetary system has since become increasingly important. In the first half of the 20th century, the banks were still mutating from a gold standard into a kind of state-owned franchise system by obtaining a state license to print money. In return, as a thank you, they are happy to finance otherwise unmanageable expenditure on over-the-top welfare benefits, inefficient bureaucracy or supposedly peace-building wars. In the background is the state central bank with a supposed independence, which provides the banks with the necessary central bank money and is also ready to intervene as a "last minute savior " when the system is, again, falling apart. The symbiosis is perfect. The state central bank and banks in general finance the state. The state and the central bank guarantee the survival of the banks that are allowed to make money themselves.

The monopolization of the monetary system and the production of money under state supervision is the most severe state intervention in a free market system of all. Money is like a bond that unites market participants worldwide and makes highly specialized, prosperous division of labor as we know it today possible. In this kind of consideration, a blatant contradiction becomes clear. If the production of goods and services is still *semi-capitalist*, the payment of these goods is carried out with a medium that has all the characteristics of a *socialist* product. In fact, money, which has been created under state regime with the elimination of all competition, and whose volume is in constant circulation, is ultimately under state control. A truly crazy idea, and anyone who's honest with themselves, must admit that this is nothing but wishful thinking—that a state money monopoly would work better than state automobile production in the GDR.

# THE WAR AGAINST GOLD

The idea that a country could withdraw from the paper money system and bind its currency to gold is without a doubt a horror scenario for politicians and supporters of large political units. But why? The EU or the US might not care if, for example, Norway, as a non-Eurozone country, bound its national currency to gold. In doing so the Norwegian Krone would massively appreciate against the Euro and US Dollar, Norwegian goods would become much too expensive for foreign countries, and Norwegian exports would surely collapse as a result; this is what's argued. The Norwegians would, in this case, hurt themselves. What does this mean for the EU, the US or the ECB?

A perfect example of why it *wouldn't* be wanted for a country, maybe a little one, to have a very strong currency bound to gold, are the events that took place in Switzerland in the 1990s.

In 1992, Switzerland joined the IMF. At that time, the vault of the Swiss National Bank contained 2,590 tons of gold, the fourth largest gold reserve in the world at that time. A lot of gold for such a small country.

In his book, *The Gold Conspiracy* (2003) Ferdinand Lips comments very critically on this matter:

*Either the real reasons for joining the IMF were not mentioned to the public and/or deliberately obscured, or the government didn't understand what it was doing at the time. [...] Despite the traditional neutrality of Switzerland, the government has consistently pursued a strategy of internationalization of Swiss politics. "We must become part of the international community" or "we cannot stay as outsiders" were the gripping "arguments" of the Federal Council and the National Bank, and they still are.*

Let's start by looking at the IMF's objectives, which anyone can read on its website:

*The IMF was created to promote international cooperation in the field of monetary policy; to facilitate the expansion and balanced growth of world trade; to promote the stability of exchange rates [...].*

Understandably, the "stability of exchange rates" proved difficult for the IMF, considering the exchange rate of two countries, one of which had a gold-backed currency, as was the case in Switzerland, and the other didn't. If the country didn't expand its money supply without gold coverage, or only to a small extent, the exchange rate ratio of both countries would be relatively stable. But without a gold standard, this wouldn't succeed, because governments, as everyone knows, like to spend more money than is available to them. One government is bound by gold, the other is not. For this reason, the currency of the country *without* gold backing will tend to depreciate against the currency of the country *with* gold backing. The comparison with the stable gold currency and devaluing paper money is naturally very unpleasant for politicians. The exchange rate becomes a reflection of their monetary policy failure and the visible and tangible indication of their debt financed spending debauchery. The disgraceful devaluation is, of course, not a good sell to the voters. And not only voters. Companies could also relocate their residence.

Because the IMF knows that, as a precaution, its *Articles of Agreement* contain Passage VI, 2b, according to which a member country is not allowed to tie its currency to gold.

Once again, from Ferdinand Lips:

*After the collapse of the Bretton Woods System, the Swiss Franc was the only currency in the world that was always backed by gold. This unique attraction and guarantee of stability made the Swiss Franc the focal point of dollar standard proponents' envy. The Swiss Franc enjoyed an attraction that the US Dollar didn't have. Its connection to gold could therefore no longer be tolerated by the builders of a future New World Order.*

In the 1990s, a real gold *war* was fought against Switzerland. The Swiss banks had to constantly defend themselves against accusations that they had absorbed property of Jews who died or went missing in World War II.

The banks carried out extensive voluntary reviews and disbursements of heirs.

Even the accusation that the Swiss government had collaborated with Hitler had to be defended. Switzerland, as small states usually do, had behaved in a neutral manner throughout the Second World War. The accusation was that the National Socialists had procured large parts of the foreign currency needed for purchases abroad by means of a gold transaction via Swiss banks. The international pressure exerted by the US in particular was immense. However, domestic political voices also strongly played around with and contributed to the fact that the Swiss central bank eventually collapsed.

With a more robust policy, Switzerland could have kept its original gold reserves. The Swiss Franc would have been an even *more* solid currency than it is today. It enjoys the reputation of a global safe-haven currency, and benefits from international comparison via its still present gold reserves, as well as from a healthy and strong economy.

# STRONG ECONOMY—STRONG CURRENCY

Critics, then as now, will argue here that a strong currency puts a country at a competitive disadvantage. It's true that, *despite* its strong currency, Switzerland has still been able to become as prosperous as it is today. The same applies to the Principality of Liechtenstein, whose national currency is the Swiss Franc. The gross domestic product per person employed is in the absolute world top ranks. In Liechtenstein, however, money is not made mainly by financial transactions, as many think. The country is highly industrialized and the main value-added branch is the manufacturing industry. And the same applies to Germany, which has always been the world's export champion despite its strong Deutsche Mark in international comparison.

Basically, Switzerland is making the same mistake today as it did more than 20 years ago. Out of problematic economic theories, various interest groups are pushing for a further weakening of the Swiss Franc, especially against the Euro, in whose currency area Switzerland sees itself embedded.

The Swiss National Bank is a central bank that has most inflated its balance sheet due to money creation in recent years; more than the ECB, the Fed or the Bank of Japan. By printing Swiss Francs and buying bonds and shares, in particular in Euros, the Central Bank is trying to prevent or at least reduce the appreciation of the Swiss Franc.

After a three-year commitment of the Swiss Franc to the Euro, which was cut in a completely surprising manner in January 2015, causing considerable difficulties for many entrepreneurs and market participants, active monetary policy is still being pursued in Switzerland.

What would have happened if Switzerland had *not* joined the IMF, had *not* sold large parts of its gold reserves and had *maintained* the gold bond of the Swiss Franc?

The external value of the Swiss Franc would certainly have risen further— not abruptly, but steadily. After all, there was no outstanding one-time event to signify this rise. The Swiss export industry could have expected its goods to become more expensive abroad. But it is precisely this competition that encourages companies to increase productivity and promotes innovation. However, since many raw materials and semi-finished products that companies need for production must also be imported, the cost of production would have been reduced. After all, with a strong currency, goods can be imported more cheaply.

Centrally planned politicians, central bankers and other bureaucrats may not be able to imagine this, but companies and the people behind them are able to adapt to such developments.

What else would have happened? The purchasing power of Swiss citizens would also have risen steadily over time. On one hand, because of the rising external value of the currency, and on the other, because, in a country that operates well, in which productivity is increased and no huge amounts of additional money are printed, the prosperity of broad social classes increases because the prices of goods and services tend to fall. As a result, many benefit from prosperity, and not only a few, as in a paper money system. Swiss consumers in particular would have benefited. Imports would have become cheaper, and what consumers can save thanks to a strong currency in their imports, they can use to buy additional domestic products and services. If the full container of fuel with imported gasoline costs only half of what you expect, you may often go out for dinner or invest in an entrepreneurial project. Small and medium-sized Swiss companies in particular would have benefited from this. Moreover, as usual in hard currency countries, capital imports and real investments would have occurred. Capital investment and lower interest rates would have fueled Switzerland even further.

Politics, on the other hand, in contrast to monetary policy, do not create prosperity. Politics can only redistribute. A policy of currency devaluation to stimulate the domestic economy favors exporting companies at the expense of the other market participants in a country, both for public and private enterprises.

# THE ELIMINATION OF CURRENCY COMPETITION

Just as before the fall of the Iron Curtain, when the West looked to the East and was able to observe in real time that socialism wasn't working and the Eastern bloc was slipping slowly but surely into bankruptcy, today, the whole world can look to Switzerland and find out how prosperous a country can become if it has gold-backed currency (good money) and if politicians have to budget and can't make debts. What a concept.

Germany had an experience similar to Switzerland. From statements by leading German and French politicians it's now known that Germany was to sacrifice the Deutsche Mark and its monetary sovereignty in exchange for German unity. The Deutsche Bundesbank, with its monetary stability oriented policy, has always been a thorn in the eye of other nations. For example, if the French government wanted a stable exchange rate with the Deutsche Mark, it had to instruct its central bank not to crank up the bank note press faster than the Bundesbank. It was no longer able to finance its public deficits to the extent that it wanted to, only to the extent of the Federal Republic. The Bundesbank's policy thus indirectly limited Paris borrowing and, ultimately, French public expenditure. It's therefore clear that the desire for German unification was, it seems, for many central-state politicians and inflationists, above all in Europe, *the* ideal opportunity to disempower a competitor in terms of money, such as Germany.

*Power corrupts and absolute power corrupts absolutely!* The historian Lord Acton (1834-1902) already knew this. Therefore, the political motto is: power-endangering competition must be eliminated and this competition prevented "whatever it takes" to use Mario Draghi's words. In order to make it more difficult for citizens to escape from currency areas and political units, they should be organized as widely as possible, preferably globally.

Even when the self-proclaimed elites feel that there is skepticism among the people, this attitude doesn't stop. In an ARD Interview in June 2016, former President Joachim Gauck said:

> The elites aren't the problem at all; at the moment, the population is the problem—one at which we're looking more closely in order to understand. Are you really afraid that you can't be Poles or Brits anymore? Is the problem that you are being taken away from your national identity? [...] So, in order to protect the idea of a unifying Europe, it is absolutely necessary to take the reluctant populations for a ride, and therefore make them thing of taking a break at the speed of acceleration of the European Union.

But whom does this policy serve? The interests of the people or the interests of political elites? Let us allow a former politician speak; he must know, after all. Thilo Sarrazin dedicates one of his own chapters in his book *Wishful Thinking* to politics and writes:

> It is inevitable that politicians serve interests. At first, he or she is only doing their job. It's also inevitable that in all of their actions they think of securing and expanding their power, too. Without power, they cannot pursue a policy. After all, it's inevitable that they act opportunistically and against better knowledge on many issues: because they make commitments from exchange transactions, because they don't want to challenge certain allies, because they are under faction and group pressure, or because they are simply thinking of their own long-term advantages.

Sarrazin shows a very realistic view here, and, it's important to consider whether it would be better for people to demand, with more vehemence, exactly the opposite of what politicians and governments want. So: not *more* EU, *less* EU. Not political *integration*, but political *decentralization*. Instead, *economic* integration and real free trade—happily global. And not *governmental* paper money, but a *competitive* money system.

# WHY LARGE STATES ARE MORE AGGRESSIVE AND SMALL STATES ARE MORE PEACEFUL

*Perhaps the dismantling of trade barriers worldwide would promote world peace more than any political Union of peoples that is shielded by trade barriers.*

*Frank Chodorov*

# PEOPLE WANT PEACE

The vast majority of people who inhabit this world are *peace-loving* people. People who want to live a happy, satisfied life in freedom, designed according to their very personal ideas of happiness. They just want to live in peace and quiet. There should be no doubt about that.

Only a small minority will find their fulfillment in a long-term dispute with the neighbors. Yes, there are quarrelsome people, that's right. But these grumblers are the exception, and moving from "arguing" to "other violence" is a significant step. Someone can even be a particularly quarrelsome contemporary, but this doesn't mean that they're ready to use violence to achieve their goals.

At first glance, these statements seem to be misguided by wars, acts of terrorism, and violence in the world—those that are current and those that are already part of history. People fight each other, atrociously, and in the worst case scenario, they kill each other. In the two World Wars alone, about 80 million people died. Countless families and existences were destroyed and countless people were expelled from their homeland.

Weapon systems were still rather simple in the 19th century, and the power of war between states was limited to the soldiers of the enemy in the nineteenth century, and this has fundamentally changed since. The economist Murray N. Rothbard (1926-1995) writes in *For a New Freedom:*

> *[...] with the emergence of centralized states and modern weapons of*
>
> *mass destruction, the slaughter of civilians, as well as conscription, became an integral part of interstate warfare.*

Above all, the chapter on the monetary system should have made it clear that the gradual release of money, which began in the last century, has made it much easier for governments to wage war and, above all, long-term wars. This is because financing via the printing press and higher government debt disguise the true cost of war. In August 1914, for example, all warring states raised the gold cover of their currencies.

Somewhere in the world there is *always* war. The people of the Middle East have been suffering more or less from war for decades. The eastern part of Ukraine is not going to find peace anytime soon. And even in the rest of Europe, as politicians always claim, peace has not prevailed for decades. During the 1990s, more than 100,000 people were killed in the Yugoslav civil war.

Politicians of all parties and of all countries let no opportunity pass to remind people of the atrocities of wars. Unfortunately, they have way too many pieces of illustrative material for this purpose on hand. When people fight for their survival, whether they are civilians or soldiers, they often commit inhuman and cruel acts, and it's not without reason that people talk about the "brutalization" of people in war. Wars create moments in which people often have no choice but to remove the character traits that distinguish them from wild animals in order to survive. If parents want to protect their children or men their wives and families, they're usually ready to do anything. In war, the rules of civilization are suspended from politics; death and destruction are guaranteed. There can be no discussion about this: any attempt to do everything possible for human beings should be made to avoid such cruel experiences.

# GOVERNMENTS START WARS, NOT THE CITIZENS

What politicians don't like to mention is that wars are always started by governments. "Simple" people don't start wars. On the contrary, they would prefer to end them immediately.

In his moving book *Silent Night*, American historian Stanley Weintraub tells the German soldier Carl Mühlegg how he carried a small Christmas tree through "No Man's Land, the guns still firing, to initiate the truce" on the front line on Christmas eve of 1914. He tells us that the gunfire didn't stop him, because "even though I was Santa Claus, with a decorated tree in my hand... I had a gun over my shoulder and a bag full of ammunition!" Having arrived on the other side, Mühlegg handed over the little Christmas tree to a British Captain.

He lit the candles on the tree and wished his soldiers, the German Nation and the whole world "peace as the Angels did in their message". Around midnight the guns and the soldiers of both armies mingled in the middle of No Man's Land between their original positions. Mühlegg describes the event with passion: "never before had I been more aware of the madness of war. [...] The ceasefire lasted for fourteen days. We were kind to each other; the reason that we started shooting each other again was because of what others decided about us."

The "others" were Generals and the governments and politicians behind them. The "others", especially the politicians, are always far away from the frontlines and from the dangers to which soldiers and civilians must expose themselves. The latter are those who have endured or perhaps have even had to die in senseless wars that they would have never begun themselves.

Why do nations war against each other at all? If one takes a look at history, one can see that wars were often preceded by economically difficult times, including in Germany in the period between the World Wars. The historian Adam Fergusson writes in his book *The End of Money:*

*Economic rescue had become the most urgent need for most people. The cost of living, poor wages, and pathetic salaries meant that they turned away from politics. Hitler alone succeeded in aligning his sails in every wind, increasingly converting the middle class to National Socialism.*

Fergusson also quotes a council member of the British Embassy in Berlin, Joseph Addison, who had seen the disaster coming, writing a letter to England in 1923:

*The population is ready to accept any system of determination or any man who demonstrates a firm will—anyone who commands with a loud, bold voice.*

The Austrian writer Stefan Zweig (1881-1942) put to paper in 1939:

*Nothing has the German people, this must be remembered again and again, so bitter, so hateful, so ready for Hitler, as inflation.*

The war in Yugoslavia was preceded by hyperinflation and a severe economic crisis. Inflation, however, is not simply caused by natural disasters. Inflation is *man*-made. But, again, not by the "simple" people, but from politicians and central bankers. Thus, the economic decline of Yugoslavia was not a disruption of free markets, but the logical consequence of decades of wasteful, socialist mismanagement, financed with ever more new debt and money created from nothing. With the progressive consumption of the capital stock, the distribution struggles between the individual republics began. The fact that Yugoslavia was so ethnically and culturally heterogeneous did not make things easier. Especially power-obsessed politicians such as the then Serbian President Slobodan Milošević called the shots; tensions often only need a spark to explode, and the killing begins.

After the end of a war, those responsible on the winning side are usually still in office, often in other governmental institutions, or they jet around the world and give highly endowed lectures. They always blame *others* for the tragedies. One could almost think that "politician" is a trained profession meant to acquire the ability to put the responsibility for any dilemma they cause into the hands of others. Or have you ever seen a politician place themselves in front of a microphone saying, "We made a serious mistake. We are to blame for this disaster."?

In this context, the author and Middle East expert Michael Lüders appeals very clearly and emphatically to his audience in his bestselling book *Who Sows the Wind:*

*Let's show toughness to those who abuse our freedom. This also includes, especially, those who sow the wind and reap the whirlwind, and not only in the Orient. The right place for them is the International Criminal Court in The Hague. On the day that charges are filed against the great corrupters and lever-pullers, or at least against some of them, notably George W. Bush, Dick Cheney, Tony Blair, Donald Rumsfeld, the phrase "Western community of values" really would come to life.*

If one looks more closely at the wars of recent decades in the Near and Middle East, one might even get the impression that wars are mostly driven by economic and power-political interests, and the scripts and fates of entire nations are written with scrutiny and calculation; long-term geopolitical plans have been forged and the scapegoats have been selected in advance. Individual tragedies are recorded as "collateral damage". When, decades later, revisionists bring the truths to light, perhaps some enlightening books or newspaper reports about these issues appear, but the history books are rarely rewritten. At least not for schools. Because they have to be approved by the politicians.

When leaders regularly throw themselves theatrically into the commemoration of war victims, reminding their citizens thereof, they should remember that their predecessors were in charge of ordering their soldiers to fight against each other. Their citizens are, by nature, almost without exception, peace-loving. They will travel to neighboring countries to spend the most beautiful weeks of the year in the location of their choice, and more and more young people will complete part of their studies at a foreign University. Students from abroad celebrate arm in arm with their fellow classmates after a short time. But not to braggingly present photos to the whole world, but just because they like each other.

# LARGE STATES ARE MORE DANGEROUS THAN SMALL STATES

But what can be done about this? What can people oppose when the "great" politicians decide to wage a Cold War, shake their sabers, provoke other nations, and end up in a war? Are people damned to powerlessness? To choose governments? There's nothing better, right?

Ludwig Erhard (1897-1977) gave us a solution. In a speech in Stockholm in 1963, he stated:

> *From my point of view, there would not be very happy times if we were to split the world back into so-called "large areas" that tried to find sufficiency within themselves. This would increase tension even within the free world. A large number of nation states may cause friction, tension and, as we have learned, even war-related entanglement in conflict of interests. But the larger the economic and political spaces with claim to power are, the more dangerous, inevitably, the opposites will become, even if, from the beginning, the general will was to promote understanding, reconciliation and cooperation.*

The Erhard approach is diametrically opposed to the current policy aspirations for a deeper political integration of Europe. If the "United States of Europe" were to become a reality, then only three major state structures would appear to someone viewing the northern hemisphere of a globe (with the exception of politically rather insignificant Canada): the United States, Russia and a united European region. *Large* powers, however, will never cease to demonstrate power and assert their claims to it. This has been observed for several years after the collapse of the Soviet Union, the Cold War was considered as ended again, more than clearly.

When Ludwig Erhard speaks of a "multitude of nation states", many politicians, including those who always quote him when it so suits them, no longer consider him up-to-date with the times. Just as politicians want to tell citizens that in a globalized world one can only exist economically from a certain size, it is also said that a nation, on its own, can impossibly defy the dangers and threats of war and terror and protect itself. Again we ask: How could the people of Switzerland, Liechtenstein or San Marino survive the two World Wars? And why does the Islamic State not attack these small defenseless states? Perhaps because they cannot or do not want to deal with fighter jets bombing targets in Syria, Iraq or Afghanistan?

Does Ludwig Erhard have the correct idea? The key to solving and preventing conflicts and aggression? That, once again, this is more easily done so in *small* units and not *large ones*? We want to investigate this now. In order to counter any possible objections: yes, there will always be power-hungry rulers, even in small countries, who want to paint their names in a negative color. Rulers who want to expand their *power*, willing to risk *everything* to do so, costing lives and property of their citizens.

There are enough examples in history. Therefore, national borders are also very important. The tighter you're drawn in, the better. It's bad enough if a despot harms its own citizens. But, fortunately, national borders also reveal themselves to politicians. And the closer the border, the easier it is for the citizens to escape unpleasant rulers.

Even if, for example, in Liechtenstein, there were to be no more prudent, peace-loving Monarch, but a despot in power, would the inhabitants of Baden-Württemberg really have to be afraid of being overrun by an army from Liechtenstein? Or would there even be a risk of Liechtenstein becoming a nuclear power? With a state budget of well below one billion Swiss Francs? Not really.

Rather, a small country must by nature be more friendly than aggressive. A small country that cannot possibly produce all the goods and services it needs must have good relations with its neighbors and other nations; it shouldn't starve its inhabitants, or even suffer from hunger at all, as the situation is, for example, in North Korea.

In addition to good trade relations, good relations in general can also be maintained by staying out of the affairs of others. Do you think your best friend would like it, in the long run, if you constantly interfered in their affairs as if you knew better? If you are asked for advice, of course, then you should try to help. But unquestioned and abrupt behavior is, for friendship, extremely counterproductive. You don't want your neighbor to interfere in the way you educate your children, do you?

In the realm of the state, this means, as in business, "laissez faire": to each one's own. What has the attempt to impose democracy on the people of the Middle East or the countries of North Africa bordering the Mediterranean brought about? Democracy? Peace? No. On the contrary, unrest and terror were the result. And there have been unprecedented, uncontrollable streams of refugees moving towards Europe.

How is it possible, then, to put political leaders and governments on a short leash in order to keep damage as low as possible if the "wrong people" get to power? This can only work if the territory they govern is as small as possible. The despot of a *small* country can therefore only cause *small* damage via aggression towards neighboring states. Alone, it lacks the means to finance a powerful, well-equipped, standing army, state-of-the-art weapons systems and weapons of mass destruction. Liechtenstein could not afford an infrastructure to maintain modern bombers. Why does Liechtenstein need an Air Force or even an aircraft carrier? If, on the other hand, large states move into war or interfere in the affairs of other nations, their power of destruction is enormous. It's to be expected that the number of victims will be higher and the clashes will continue for a longer period of time.

According to the arguments of large-state representatives, smaller nations would have to use more money per capita on their defense in order to be able to outdo the military of larger states. Finally, the latter could play their economies of scale against the former. The small states would have to worry more about their security and defense than the large ones. To see that the opposite is the case and that it's not about defense, but about power, one must only take a look at the military spending in 2015 of selected countries.

For better comparability, the figures are all given in US dollars; the figures are from the Peace Research Institute Sipri in Stockholm. According to this list, the Swiss government spent just over $5 billion on national defense. That's $609 for every Swiss. In France, a nuclear power, the military budget for the year was almost 61 billion US dollars, which is 944 US dollars per capita, almost 49 percent more than for a Swiss person.

The military budget of the great Superpower of the United States in 2015 amounted to an incredible 595 billion dollars. Every US-American is thus responsible for an incredible $ 1,850 in military expenditure—more than twice as much as the French government and three times as much as the Swiss government spends per capita. Where are the economies of scale, the so-called scale effect? Military expenditure related to the size of a nation seems to have its own laws.

If one were to break down the Swiss national defense budget to possibly politically independent (there are 26 in number) that would still be about 192 million US dollars per canton, but militarily this means "there's no prize to be won". And that's good.

A thought that's also pressing: what would the citizens of a country say with a comparatively high military budget if there were never any missions for the military? The soldiers would sit in the barracks, maybe occasionally hold a drill, but otherwise only burning tax money? This would be the same as holding a fire station with five fire engines in a community of 500, although something might burn somewhere in the village once a year. You don't have to be a conspiracy theorist to come to the idea that a military apparatus going beyond national defense from time to time needs an effort to provide arguments for its *raison d'être*. And not only when it comes to alleged peacekeeping measures in the Hindu Kush region.

Leopold Kohr formulates this context provocatively:

*An army that is so carefully and so zealously kept in motion must ultimately be put to use even if, originally, by its establishment, only relatively cheap job creation was intended. This is still evident from the fact that the common soldier's pay to this day is more in line with unemployment allowance than more usually accepted wages. Still, it does need to be used from time to time, if only out of concern that their loved ones might otherwise lose their self esteem when they finally realize they are nothing more than nogood consumers in society.*

# SMALL STATES ARE MORE PEACEFUL THAN LARGE STATES

Big states are like bulls in china shops; they will definitely be dangerous, even without evil intent. All one has to do is tip the balance a little or even succumb to the temptation to contribute to "big politics." Small, on the other hand, is refined and peaceful. There are good reasons for this.

A statement attributed to the French economist and politician Frédéric Bastiat (1801-1850) puts it in a nutshell: *if goods do not cross borders, soldiers will.* The reason why smaller states are known for peacemaking is hidden precisely within this sentence. Small states *must* pursue a policy of open borders. War hinders and disrupts the free movement of goods. And the movement of goods is vital for small countries today. Self-sufficiency is not an option. You can't produce everything by yourself; you have to import from your neighbors—as do distant countries. You have to sign up for free trade. Small states are much more dependent on undisturbed trade than large states, in whose vast territories many goods can be produced reasonably efficiently. Liechtenstein has no oil, gas and coal deposits, and no car factories or extensive fishing areas. Russia and the United States do. Great empires can therefore rather afford to shut themselves off in a war.

The general free trade which is compulsory for today's small states is conducive to peace. Because free trade makes it possible to obtain important goods through voluntary exchanges. If, on the other hand, the borders are closed and access to vital raw materials is blocked or threatened, then, as in the past, many soldiers begin to move. Small states make the world more peaceful.

Big states are connected to big politics—world politics. This is the claim of those with great power, and this claim is also developed by the EU, which wants to see itself on an equal footing with Russia, China and especially the

USA. But with world politics come new problems, which don't arise in small states at all. The political leaders with great powers have the opportunity, and often the desire, to enter into history books. And suddenly, at the other end of the world, people are mixed up in the affairs of completely unknown people. For example, US presidents who have not pushed their country into war aren't usually known as "war presidents" and are often considered as weak presidents in the historical perspective.

Could you imagine throwing a bomb at your neighbor's house? An absurd idea! However, what we would never do to our neighbors happens on a daily basis if only enough distance is in between. The US military uses remote-controlled drones to bomb people in a house on the other side of the globe. People you have never seen or never will see alive, with whom you aren't economically connected and whose language or culture is foreign to you. It seems the threshold of violence falls with the mental distance *from* and the foreignness *to* the victim. It follows that the smaller the states, the more similar, more familiar, economically dependent and culturally integrated the neighboring states tend to be. This makes them more peaceful than the giant states that pursue global politics all over the world.

# DISCRIMINATION AGAINST MINORITIES

There is another problem with large states. As we have already seen, people have different goals and values in life. In small communities, in family, in towns and villages, perhaps even in regions, one can fairly easily compensate. However, the larger the state structures, the more difficult it becomes to reconcile the heterogeneous interests of the citizens. Then, the socalled "minorities" emerge, who no longer see their needs represented, who are "discriminated against", who might want a different language of instruction or a different dress code in schools, who want to commit to other holidays or simply want equal access to power. Discrimination against minorities becomes a source of conflict and even wars when other powers interfere.

In the 19th century, the Prussian government discriminated against the Polish minority on their territory by trying to enforce German as the language of instruction. This was not exactly beneficial to the harmony between Germany and Poland. Another example is the discrimination against the Sudetenland German minority in Czechoslovakia after the First World War. The disadvantage of German companies in government contracts, the closure of German schools and the displacement of German officials from the public service provided Adolf Hitler with a pretext for military intervention. In the Polish side of things, there was also a policy of "de-Germanization." Hitler also justified his attack on Poland with the protection of the German minorities and therefore triggered the Second World War. The following applies: if each minority has its own state, the potential for conflict is reduced. And the larger the states, the more likely they are to include minorities whose wishes are not respected by the central government. This oppression of minorities endangers peace.

# PROTECTION OF THE POPULATION BY THE GOVERNMENT?

Estimates of the number of victims of the Second World War are sometimes far apart, usually between 50 and 65 million people dead. Of them, however, only a part of this number perished in direct battles. The majority of the victims were civilians killed off the battlefield: by genocide and war crimes, hunger and epidemics. In fact, fighting in itself was not the greatest threat to people in the 20th century. The greatest danger in the end has always been the state – be it one's own or that of a stranger.

In his monumental study *Death by Government*, the US political scientist R. J. Rummel (1932-2014) estimates the number of people killed by governments between 1900 and 1987 to be at a tremendous 170 million. This figure is far higher than the number of war deaths that Rummel estimates to be 34 million in the same period. These 170 million people were killed through genocide, indiscriminate mass murder, or political persecution, shot, stabbed, burned, drowned, hanged, buried alive, tortured to death, starved, or worked to death. Helpless citizens and foreigners.

Who leads this list of political mass murder? That's right: the giant states. Lonely at the top of the list is the Soviet Union, which, according to average estimate, murdered nearly 62 million people in the period studied. In second place follows Communist China, having killed about 35 million people of its own population (1949-87). The National Socialist mass killers account for about 21 million people. China, in turn, ranks fourth with 10 million victims during the period of the nationalist regime of Chiang Kai-shek (1928-49). These are then followed by the large states of Japan (1936-45), China (192349; with the victims of the Maoist civil war), Cambodia (1975-79), the Ottoman Empire (1909-18), Vietnam (1945-87), Poland (1945-48), Pakistan

(1958-87) and Yugoslavia (1944-87), which together have an estimated 19 million deaths on their conscience. No sign of small states. In the list of the most murderous regimes, which is based on the percentage of the population murdered per year, small states are also absent. Here, the Khmer Rouge Regime leads to Turkey Atatürk, to Yugoslavia and to post-war Poles. Not Singapore, not Hong Kong, not San Marino, not Liechtenstein, not Switzerland.

In the 20th century the greatest danger to life and health was in the form of large states. And why do the governments of small states not kill their populations on a grand scale? Small political units simply cannot act as brutally against their own population as large ones. They'd be emptied immediately. Because they cannot produce everything themselves, small states must create a certain openness to the rest of the world. Their borders would be open and close to each other.

# IN THE DEFENSE OF SMALL STATES

If one imagines small political units, as we have described in the chapters before, critics will argue that for countries on the scale of, say, San Marino, it would be utopian to maintain their own army, even for defense purposes only. This is, of course, correct; yes, San Marino has no army—only a ceremonial guard—and has concluded an agreement with Italy that the defense of San Marino is guaranteed. Iceland also has no own army and has entered into a defense alliance with NATO. In return, the country leases clearly defined areas for free to NATO, where military exercises can be conducted. Also, Monaco has no military and, like San Marino, has only a Castle Guard, which serves more or less as a tourist attraction. The defense of Monaco is taken over by France in the event of an emergency. And the island of Mauritius also has no military—only a special unit and a Coast Guard.

In all these examples, it should be noted, by the way, that none of these countries in the past have shown any form of aggression against other nations. Why? They can't afford it at all. On the one hand, because they are too weak, and on the other, because they depend on nations for reasons other than being trading partners. And because they don't want to end up like North Korea.

But, how can we address the argument that the threat to the world today cannot be overcome by a small country alone? At this point we can look back into history, more precisely to the Hanseatic League. From 12th to the 17th century, numerous cities organized their defense together and were thus extremely successful. After all, the Hanseatic League survived five centuries and existed longer than the United States has.

Among the members of the Hanseatic League were cities such as Lübeck, Hamburg, Bremen, Stralsund, Rostock, Wismar, Cologne, Dortmund, Lüneburg, Münster, Gdańsk, Greifswald, Braunschweig and many more. In emergencies, they also cooperated militarily, once defeating the King of Denmark several times, who wanted to restrict their rights. In particular, they worked together politically and economically, but remained completely independent. The Hanseatic League didn't constitute a monopoly in which there was any form of compulsory membership or an obligation to use certain services. The culture flourished and, through its free trade, many of its members gained great economic wealth, which can still be seen today in the magnificent buildings in the venerable Hanseatic cities. Why not revive this great Hanseatic tradition today? With politically independent cities like Lübeck, Bremen, Wismar, Rostock, etc.?

Critics of our theory will argue that the comparison is "medieval" and not transferable to our globalized world with all its dangers and threats. But who would invade an independent Münster or Stralsund today?

We don't want to use the example of the Hanseatic League much longer, but so much has been said: the combination of numerous cities offered a powerful defense in the event of an attack. This was also true for the South German Township Association which consisted of 89 cities and was able to set up a force of 10,000 soldiers if required. The Rheinland Township Association in the 13th century, with 59 cities (including Mainz, Worms, Basel, Strasbourg, Frankfurt, Speyer, Aachen, Duisburg) also cooperated militarily and maintained their own Rhine fleet. The Swabian Township Association of 1379 was overseen by the leadership of Ulm, which entered into alliances with the South German Township Association and the Swiss Imperial Township Association, and also shows how independent cities can join together militarily.

In recent history, too, there is an example of how cities and regions joined forces to form defense alliances: the German Confederation. It existed from 1815 to 1866. At this point, to list all its members would exceed the scope of this book. Only this: in addition to the Austrian Empire, the kingdoms of Prussia, Bavaria, Saxony, Hanover, and Württemberg, as well as other Dukes and Duchies and free cities belonged to it. There was no compulsory membership; over the years there were new members, while others left the Confederation. The federal army, which consisted of contingents of the individual members, was organized in such a way that it was defensive but not offensive. The main purpose of the Confederation may also have been to ensure a functioning defense against large and centralized France.

But critics would also want to sweep these examples off the table, because the challenges of globalization and the threat of terrorism have since been added.

Let us therefore focus on the way in which protection is organized in other areas that we encounter on a *daily* basis, where people are *also* at risk of life, limb and property. For this purpose, let's consider the organization of police or firefighters. The tasks of both police, firefighters and technical assistance include *defending* citizens from dangers and protecting them, not acting aggressively against them. For example, in small communities of 1,000 inhabitants, police offices are rarely found, because they are simply not required there. The same applies to the organization of firefighters. Having a firefighting service only makes sense when there is a certain size to a municipality or city. And even if a community has a small fire department, it doesn't mean it's going to have to deal with every threatening scenario. In such situations, fire departments from neighboring locations come to help, or special equipment is provided, for example, a breathing apparatus for a large fire in a chemical factory or special cutters to help in traffic accidents. Police forces are also pulled together in one place when the officials there are numerically understaffed or technically overwhelmed.

Transferred to a scenario with small political units, for example, if the state of Bavaria broke away from the Federal Republic of Germany, it would have a Bavarian constitution that would be formulated as a constitution of a full state and could join together for the purpose of common defense with Switzerland. Although Bavaria could, of course, maintain its own army, both countries could also jointly organize tasks and therefore make use of synergy effects. The Swiss defense budget amounts to 4.6 billion Euros. Is it realistic that Bavaria could raise such an amount to finance a common military, the only task of which would be to protect the people, but not to interfere in other countries' affairs? Where could Bavaria take the money? Well, that shouldn't be a problem, given that in 2015 the Free State alone had to pay 5.5 billion Euros into the national fiscal equalization plan. In other words, the payment to the federal fiscal equalization exceeds the entire Swiss military budget by about 20 percent. But that's not all. Since, in the case of being autonomous, Bavaria could also create other taxes on its own. According to Article 106 (3) of the German Basic Law, the federal government and the States each receive 42.5 percent of the income tax and assessed income tax revenue (the remaining 15 percent goes to the municipalities). In 2015, this was 18.4 billion euros. This means that Bavaria, if it were to be dissolved by the Federal Republic of Germany, could own the federal share of 18.4 billion. If you add the 5.5 billion that Bavaria had to pay as a federal fiscal equalization in 2015, you get extra revenues of 23.9 billion euros. We're even disregarding potential additional revenue from sales tax. Their distribution is governed by a Federal law and varies from time to time. We also don't want to over calculate here, because in the case of becoming autonomous, certain expenses would be borne by Bavaria. However, a strong army of its own or joint defense with Switzerland seems no impossibility with an additional revenue of almost 24 billion Euros. There would probably still be room for juicy tax cuts. So, instead of redeeming the funds via fiscal equalization and taxes to the federal government, for Berlin to finance the federal military to defend Bavarian Freedom in the Hindu Kush and join in the Syrian war after the opening of the Bavarian borders, Bavaria could just as well, for the money, take its own defense in hand.

Bavaria could therefore kill several birds with one stone by splitting from the Federal Republic: it could regain the sovereignty it lost with its entry into the centralist single state of the new German Reich in 1871, organize its own National Defense and even lower taxes, which could lead to further prosperity gains for the citizens. An army capable of attack would not need Bavaria – we simply assume that a Bavarian state government wouldn't intend to take over its neighbor, Austria. And if the Austrians saw fit to invade Bavaria, and the Bavarian soldiers became overwhelmed by the attack, the Swiss would come to their aid. You think that would be a naive idea and the threat of terrorism would not be so easily mastered? Question: How many terrorist attacks have there been in Iceland, Liechtenstein, Andorra, Tirol, Vorarlberg, Bern, Aargau, Ticino...?

Just as in a free market, the supply of goods according to the needs and preferences of the market participants are organized, and would unite small nations, and political entities to organize their defense. As the preferences and needs of people differ, so too do the needs of nations. Small political units seeking to actively exchange goods with other nations—without customs barriers and other trade restrictions—do not show any aggression towards their neighbors. Their need for protection is therefore far less than that of a nation which is overly active in world politics and which claims to interfere everywhere.

As in a free market, the choices would be crucial. If Bavaria didn't fulfil its idea of security in the joint defense alliance with Switzerland, for whatever reason, it could turn to Tyrol, which is, today, a federal state of Austria. Or Tyrol, Bavaria, and Switzerland could organize their protection against possible aggressors together. There are no limits to imagination. And if a region believed itself not to need protection at all, that's also good. Liechtenstein, for example, doesn't have its own army, nor does it have any agreement with neighboring countries in a defense alliance.

Threats and dangers to a country usually arise only through aggression against other nations and through interference in their internal affairs. Consistent neutrality, as practiced in Liechtenstein, as well as friendly behavior aimed at a lively exchange of goods, reduce the threatening situation and thus the need for protection and the expense of National Defense.

Now one could object: but what happens to a small country that has a militaristic and aggressively large neighbor, who has little interest in consistent neutrality and lively exchange of goods? What about Russia, for example, the giant neighbor of the Baltic States? Yes, no question, this is indeed a big problem.

NATO, against all commitments, has put more and more pressure on Russia. The situation is tense, also because of the Russian minorities in these countries. Small countries like the Baltic States would probably *have* to form a defense alliance. Not only among themselves but also with others. In doing so, they would turn into a stronger alliance rather than a weaker one. They would also have to try to satisfy their minorities, if necessary, with a secession, i.e. a further reduction.

However, the giant neighbor will first have to justify an attack against his own people, which is not easy with strict neutrality from the small neighbor, stemming from harmonious trade agreements. But who knows: maybe the "Russian bear" is also much more peaceful than commonly assumed, and the picture that is mostly painted of him doesn't do justice to his real nature. Instead of carrying out large-scale military maneuvers at the Russian front door, the West should simply trust in Russia, without armies. An honest attempt would be worth it in any case.

Under no circumstances should a joint defense alliance in any form be political. It should focus solely on military defense tasks—otherwise peace is in danger again. It would be strictly forbidden for such an alliance to interfere with internal affairs of its member countries or with those of nations outside the alliance. NATO, which was founded after World War II as a purely "collective defense alliance," has nevertheless become independent over the decades. Meanwhile, they claimed the right to intervene even *without* a mandate from the United Nations (UN) in areas of crisis and international conflicts. "Peace Operations" is the name that illegal wars are known by. It has nothing to do with mere *defense*. And with the ever-tried argument of prevention alone, much harm can be done, and this argument can justify virtually anything. Not only that preventive inputs and attacks provoke unwanted counter-reactions. Even *talking about* possible threat scenarios makes any disarmament talks more difficult. And disarmament must be the goal of every peace-loving person. Disarmament down to a level that meets one's own defense.

Critics may refuse this argument as a utopian attempt to free the world from wars and make it more peaceful. However, in our eyes, a goal is "Utopian" only when there are theoretical reasons which suggest it is infeasible. No one is denying that there is practical resistance and political and economic interests that stand in the way of a more peaceful world. But this doesn't mean that the goal is unattainable. As we have seen, there are viable ways to curtail political power that, in its dimension and abuse, ultimately makes the difference between war and peace. A way to a peaceful world is through smaller political units. Of course, something must change in people's minds first. One must come to the belief that small is fine, efficient and peaceful. And they must be encouraged not to succumb to political propaganda, that "largeness" is now the alternative. With this book we would like to make a small contribution to this thought process.

The size of State plays *the* decisive role in the circumcision of political power, and a given size is not immutable. Borders are not given by God and can also be changed and re-drawn by peaceful means. Who knows what would have been if the then Prague government had engaged in confrontation with the Slovak pro-independence activists? Unlike in Yugoslavia, the country's politicians, especially Václav Klaus, wisely and prudently entered into joint discussions. Without violence, the dissolution of Czechoslovakia and the founding of the republics of the Czech Republic and Slovakia took place on January 1st, 1993.

Madrid, Rome and London should be just as obvious as examples, if Catalan, North Italy, South Tyrol, or Scots don't lose patience with their central governments. A government's stubborn behavior unnecessarily provokes violence. No. Small states are by nature more peaceful and less dangerous. Immoral, low-power politicians would then have fewer opportunities to satisfy their instincts. Those who want to secure peace must refrain from large-scale structures. Less is often more. And smaller is safer.

# EPILOGUE:

# TWO SCENARIOS FOR THE FUTURE

# SCENARIO 1:

## *The United States of Europe*

Mr. Michel had just frustratedly turned off his TV. A meeting between the U.S. President and the President of the USE (United States of Europe) had been airing on the evening news. Both nations had come to agree on far-reaching negotiations in the past few days. Top officials would now work out the details and, soon, the agreements would enter into force, a spokesman said. Looking at the cameras with confident smiles, the two Heads of State shook hands and agreed to harmonize all tax directives, to introduce a special tax to finance climate protection, and to substantiate imports from other countries that weren't prepared to adjust their taxes to align with massive fines and other trade sanctions that would come into play.

The most controversial point was the Health-Flexi-Tax, the European President said in the interview. But they were able to agree with the USA in the end and were very happy about it. If, in the future, the price of sugar fell and the prices of chocolate, ice cream and other health-threatening sweets fell, as well, the sugar tax would automatically increase. The additional revenues generated by this would be consistently invested in the expansion of the state health system and the expansion of Veggie-Day, offered nationwide and free of charge. In addition, subsidizing the purchase of bicycles would soon be implemented, so that the citizens would move and exercise more. In cities with a population of 10,000 or more, the purchase of a monthly ticket for local transport was to be made mandatory for each adult resident in order to relieve the cities of car traffic. Sometimes, people need to be forced to find their happiness, said the President. Politics knows what's good for people.

It was at this point that Mr. Michel had turned off his TV. Although he was home alone, he scoffed loudly. He leaned back in his chair and stared at the ceiling.

He was, and he was recently becoming aware of this, just like the vast majority of European citizens affected by the phrases and propaganda of politicians. He used to believe that a single country, even Germany, could no longer exist in the world on its own—on one hand because of the challenges of globalization, and on the other, because of international terrorist threats.

The EU states were eventually merged into the United States of Europe. Mr. Michel had accepted this development at that time. It seemed to him that progress would have come sooner or later anyway. In some countries there were protests in the months before the decision, but the participants were dismissed by politicians and by the media as crazy and petty. The EU countries that had not yet adopted the Euro had to decide: *remain or leave*.

Meanwhile, Brussels regulated and controlled *everything*. The national parliaments still met, but had little to report. All skills were centralized in Brussels. More than 300,000 civil servants worked there at present.

More and more cases of corruption and waste had come to light in Brussels, and billions of Euros were always involved. Someone being held accountable was unheard of, although large sums of money for pointless projects were spent anyway. Investments were regularly justified on the grounds of climate protection, the improvement of infrastructure, better education opportunities, the creation of jobs or the ever-expressed platitude "social justice." Critics who dared to contradict each other had to prepare themselves for campaigns that bordered on reputation murder.

There were also massive changes in the field of defense. The German Defense Force was history and had turned into the UEA (United European Army). The EU's relationship with Russia had deteriorated dramatically after Ukraine joined the EU. There were always minor incidents and battles on the border with Russia. The number of nuclear warheads had increased significantly after years of disarmament after the turn of the century.

At each corner, public safety cameras had been installed. More and more terrorist attacks took place in larger European cities, but people somehow got used to it all; there seemed to be no alternatives. There had also been a sharp increase in crime in recent years. But one didn't have to be afraid to be robbed of their cash: except for coins used for the settlement of microtransactions, cash had been abolished and, immediately afterwards, a general negative interest on bank deposits of minus 2 percent was introduced. This negative interest rate should have been applied for one year, but the scheme had already been extended twice.

In the city where Mr. Michel lived, many businessmen and entrepreneurs had given up. Including some of his acquaintances. More and more regulations, and more bureaucracy, had made their businesses unprofitable. Many shops in the inner cities were empty. Large commercial chains and companies found it easier to cope with the ever more bureaucratic rules in Brussels. The effort to meet them was only made by large corporations. And with loans at interest rates of close to zero, they raised oversized markets in the commercial areas in the cities, putting pressure on more and more retailers, who ultimately had to stop working. Subtenants for their properties were often found only in operators of mobile phone shops or nail salons, if any.

Old-age poverty had become more and more prevalent. The Baby Boomer generation was now retired, but their life insurance policies, savings plans and other traditional, conservative investments had not generated enough to maintain the standard of living in their old age due to zero and negative interest rates. Millions of citizens were affected. Inner cities made an increasingly bleak impression, purchasing power was lacking in every corner, and even money for the maintenance of property was increasingly lacking.

A good friend of Mr. Michel, formerly an owner of a sports business, had once opened his heart to him a few years ago at a birthday party. Maybe he had had one glass of wine too much and was accordingly talkative. As of ten employees, Brussels had decided that entrepreneurs would have to hire at least one migrant, and there were even subsidies for hiring other volunteers. He had nothing against foreigners, and, especially, not when he knew they were at war in their countries of origin, he understood completely why they fled. But if they couldn't speak German and had no education, his acquaintance complained, he couldn't hire them, as they couldn't contribute to the finances of his business. Last year he had had to declare insolvency.

Mr. Michel himself worked at a large company in the field of Controlling. His company had recently been taken over, after the company in which he had originally started had also been taken over a few months earlier. The employees no longer knew what exact ownership arrangements were in place. "Some hedge fund," most people said. In fact, it didn't matter, because the individual employee didn't play any role any more. His work as a Controller made him aware, every day, of what Management was up to. Of course, a company must make profits, Mr. Michel knew, but replacement investments also had to be made. But that wasn't a point on the Directors' to-do list. The focus was on the highest possible dividend payments to shareholders and generous bonuses for managers. He was just glad that he didn't have to pay for it if the results of his department didn't match the Management's expectations.

Over the last few years, Mr. Michel had often played with the idea of leaving Europe. Just going away. But where? In order to move to another country, where one could still live freely, pay less in taxes, or simply live a less defeated life, one would have to move thousands of kilometers away. In addition, Brussels had introduced a withholding tax of an entire annual salary if one moved. How would he cope with that? Practically no one could afford that.

One of Michel's acquaintances had made it to Switzerland in 2018. For a long time, however, he wasn't able to enjoy his new freedom. When Britain finally left the EU after the Brexit decision, the British immediately agreed on a completely free movement of goods with Switzerland. He could still remember well when the British Prime Minister presented the treaty at a press conference. His acquaintance had sent him the link to a live broadcast on the Internet, with a note that he should see it. It wasn't reported on public television in Germany. The free trade agreement between the United

Kingdom and Switzerland was exactly one page long. The heads of government of both countries were visibly proud of the result.

Shortly thereafter, however, Brussels began to put pressure on Switzerland. The EU leadership expressed it more diplomatically, but the demand for Switzerland was: "either you join the EU or we cancel all bilateral trade agreements with you." At this time, forty percent of Swiss exports went to the EU. The outrage in Switzerland was initially huge. But the threat was just a rough draft for those political forces in Switzerland whose goal had always been to make the Swiss Confederacy part of the EU. The atmosphere was tremendously tense, and the Swiss Franc, competing against the Euro, played into their hands. A referendum soon followed. An unprecedented propaganda campaign—it was suspected that it had received massive financial support from Brussels—hit the Swiss people hard. With a significant two-thirds majority, the Swiss voted to join the USE. As of last year, Switzerland had become an independent state.

# SCENARIO 2:

## *Returning to What's Small*

Mr. Tell stood on his balcony and looked out over the city. Five years ago, there had been nothing here but a green meadow. At that time, Titus City had had about 8,000 inhabitants: small but nice, one could say. About 40 years earlier, Mr. Tell had been in this area for the first time when he took a holiday with his parents in the Thuringian Forest. Never in his life, he thought to himself then, would he have wanted to call this God-forgotten region his home. If the Euro hadn't been introduced, he might not have been standing on this balcony now, enjoying the sunset with a glass of red wine. In retrospect, that monetary union was, so to speak, the beginning of the end.

The years of euphoria after the introduction of the Euro had passed quickly by with the beginning of the financial crisis. Then followed the disillusionment. The crisis brought to light all the bad investments, not only in Southern Europe, which had created ever-cheaper credit money out of thin air. For years, governments had been using bail-out packages and investment programs, and the European Central Bank, with zero interest rates and sovereign debt monetization, to keep alive the biggest monetary experiment of all time. European integration was driven forward with all possible power, but in the end all efforts were in vain. Political acts of desperation such as negative interest rates and helicopter money made the turmoil even worse. Eventually, the crisis made its final journey and it came, as it had to come: a depression worse than the 1930s took Europe in its grip and, consequently, the entire world economy.

After the British had consequently left the EU, the total chaos waiting for the UK that was so often spoken about was interestingly absent—the opposite of what the EU leaders had predicted. Britain opened up to trade unilaterally around the world, but could not escape the effects of the global depression. However, the British did not quite catch it as bad as the EU countries.

Once again, it was from Brussels that the citizens were promised salvation. The rich must now show solidarity, it was said, when the unemployment rates shot up. In practice, this meant that taxes on wealthy people in the EU were massively increased. To the surprise of many middle-class people, they were also included on this list of wealthy individuals. Moreover, the richer EU countries were expected to support the poorer ones even more, so that the imbalances within the EU wouldn't be too large. Within these respective nations, more and more was redistributed and the people of power always expected more and more. In individual countries, for example, the economically stronger federal states or provinces were expected to finance the weaker ones until the crisis was over. The word "solidarity" replaced the word "social" at the top of the scale of words most commonly used by politicians.

But fancy words from the mouths of politicians did not seem to convince the people of Europe, but rather to provoke them, understandably, especially those who were once again expected to foot the bill. There had been massive, unprecedented protests, first in Catalonia, soon afterwards in northern Italy, in which the people looked up to the British and the path they had chosen. It seemed as if all citizens were literally going to the streets; Mr. Tell had also taken part in the protest marches. He was satisfied with his commitment. He had been involved in civic debates, brought informative material to people, had shared infographics on the Internet, and had enlightened his family and friends on the matter. He had been one of many. He had become part of and had helped develop a self-reinforcing, ever-faster-growing movement. Then, people stopped giving up. A competition of ideas was underway, and the better ideas began to assert themselves. Driven by visionary politicians who fought for years to split their regions, governments soon felt that they could no longer handle the situation. When it became clear that the protests of the Catalans and the northern Italians could be crowned with success, the citizens of Bavaria and Baden-Württemberg also took to the streets. The Scots did the same.

Regional movements sprang up like mushrooms from the ground. The Hanse was resurrected. At annual meetings, several venerable trade cities demanded their independence.

The governments probably gave in to the secessionist endeavors of many regions and cities in the end, because economically everything was terrible anyway and they assumed that things couldn't get any worse. The main reason, however, was that they were afraid of the protesters. They would have needed to bring the angry people back under control.

Then, everything changed relatively quickly. At first, the northern Italians split from the rest of the country and proclaimed independence. The year after, the Catalans did the same, saying "Adéu, Espanya!" Only two years later, Bavaria and Baden-Württemberg set out to become autonomous. Shortly thereafter, a whole series of old Hanseatic cities followed suit. Closing their eyes to reality, the Brussels elites threatened: the 'apostates' would be excluded from any bilateral trade with the EU! But that didn't deter people from their goals. The threats of Brussels were ultimately only hot air. Everybody knew that by now. Whether Catalonia, Bavaria, Baden-Württemberg, Northern Italy or the Hanseatic Cities: all of them were economically extremely important trading hubs or strong industrial regions whose products the rest of the EU couldn't refuse without massively harming themselves.

It didn't take too long for the newly created nations to settle into their new statuses even more economically positively than before. The new governments reduced taxes for private individuals and businesses. Investments and innovations immediately increased, as did envious external views. In more and more states in Germany, in the departments, regions and cities of other nations, these voices also grew louder: to go the way of the 'apostates' and not to let everything be dictated centrally by Brussels and the respective capitals.

As expected, the last shreds of confidence in the Euro were lost. In any case, not much was left of its original purchasing power. The remaining economies in the EU were hit again. The governments of the now independent countries, however, had already, wisely, approved private currencies as additional means of payment. Gold and silver circulated in electronic form. Bitcoin was also used more and more often. The economic chaos caused by the collapse of the Euro was therefore limited, because there were still functioning tools of exchange.

Slowly, but surely, the map of Europe resembled a patchwork carpet; like Germany in Goethe's time. Each new small nation, region or independent city consistently pursued a policy of free trade with other nations. More and more countries focused on what they did best, looked at what their neighbors did and imitated them, and avoided mistakes that others had wrongly made in the past.

Since the collapse of the Euro, funds for subsidies for nonsense projects had practically ceased to exist, and social benefits had been reduced. As a result, poverty migration became almost non-existent; the borders could be opened and trade flourished.

The lack of subsidies meant that, in structurally poor regions, prices for real estate, land and property fell. This is also the case in the now newly independent "Thuringia". The local government had initially hesitated; then, a resourceful and visionary entrepreneur approached them with the proposal to provide a piece of land on which to found a private city. The bureaucrats could not imagine the idea that was already planned and completed within the visionary's mind. He referred to a private city he had founded ten years ago on a part of the state territory of Honduras. In the meantime, 10,000 people from all over the world had come to live there. *The cities are just for the rich; an average citizen couldn't afford to live there, something we shouldn't support*, critics said of the concept. However, a flourishing economy had developed around the private city in Honduras. Service providers, craftsmen, contractors and many more industries had settled around the, then, first ever "Private City". Thousands of jobs had been created in a region that had just recently been dominated by crime, unemployment and poverty. The reference model finally convinced the government of Thuringia. A politician said in an Interview: "Perhaps our countryside is beginning to bloom, as Chancellor Kohl promised at the time to the citizens." So, Titus City was formed.

Mr. Tell looked down from the balcony at the busy hustle and bustle in the streets. Thinking over the last few decades, he rejoiced not only at the fact that political power was barely playing any roles any more, and most of all, that the world had become more peaceful. As a result of political dissociation, NATO had lost massive influence. Even the US, which had enough to deal with in the wake of the economic crisis, had become more peaceful in its foreign policy. No wonder, after all, as they had been losing one ally after another. The threat posed by Russia, which began to build up in the years following the turn of the last millennium, also emerged as propaganda, just like so much other material.

The political policy in Russia was far from being described as "liberal". However, in view of developments in the West, Russian leadership had no choice but to give its citizens more and more freedom.

More and more people in more and more regions and cities around the world came to the conclusion that small states present big possibilities.

# SOURCES

Bandulet, Bruno, *Beuteland*, 2016, Rottenburg: Kopp

Eckermann, Johann Peter, *Gespräche mit Goethe*, 1999, Munich: dtv

Erhard, Ludwig, Stockholm speech, 23.03.1963, in: *Gedanken aus fünf Jahrzehnten*, in 1988, Düsseldorf: Econ

Fergusson, Adam, *The End of Money*, 3. Edition 2012, Munich, Germany: FinanzBuch Publishing

Hans-Adam II Prince of Liechtenstein, *Der Staat im dritten Jahrtausend*, 2. Edition 2014, Triesen/Liechtenstein: van Eck Publishing

Hayek, Friedrich von, *Die verhängnisvolle Anmaßung: Die Irrtümer des Sozialismus*, 1988, Tübingen: Mohr

Hoppe, Hans-Hermann, *Demokratie. Der Gott, der keiner ist*, 2003, Waltrop: Manuscript

Hoppe, Hans-Hermann, *Der Wettbewerb der Gauner*, 2012, Berlin: Holzinger Publishing

Hoppe, Hans-Hermann, Small is Beautiful and Efficient: the Case For Secession, in *Telos*, 1996, 95101

Kohr, Leopold, *Die überentwickelten Nationen*, 2003, Salzburg: Otto Müller Publishing

Kohr, Leopold, *"Small is beautiful"*, 1995, Vienna: Deuticke

Kohr, Leopold, *Wenne Staat*, 2004, Salzburg: Otto Müller Verlag

Lips, Ferdinand, *Die Goldverschwörung*, 2006, Rottenburg: Kopp

Lüders, Michael, *Wer den Wind sät Was westliche Politik im Orient anrichtet*, 2015, München: C.H. Beck

Mises, Ludwig von, *Liberalismus,* 1927, Jena: Gustav Fischer Publishing

Mises, Ludwig von, *Nationalökonomie. Theorie des Handelns und Wirtschaftens*, 1940, Geneva: Editions Union Geneva

Paul, Ron, *Swords into Plowshares*, 2015, Clute, TX: Ron Paul Institute for Peace and Prosperity

Polleit, Thorsten (Ed.), *Ludwig von Mises: Leben und Werk für Einsteiger*, 2013, München: FinanzBuch Publishing

Raico, Ralph, Das europäische Wunder in Europa: Die Wiederentdeckung eines großen Erbes, in: Pierre Bessard (Hrsg.), *Europa – Die Wiederentdeckung eines großen Erbes*, 2015, Zürich: Edition Liberales Institute

Rothbard, Murray N.,*Für eine neue Freiheit*1, 2012, edition g
Rummel, Rudolph Joseph, *Death by Government*, 1994, New Brunswick: Transaction Publishers

Sarrazin, Thilo, *Wunschdenken*, 2016, Munich: DVA
Scharnagl, Wilfried, *Bayern kann es auch allein*, 2012, Berlin: Quadriga

Taleb, Nassim Nicholas, *Antifragilität*, 2013, München: Knaus
Vaubel, Roland, Der Wettbewerb der Staaten als Erfolgsgeheimnis Europas: Eine Theoriegeschichte, in: Pierre Bessard (Hrsg.), *Europa – Die Wiederentdeckung eines großen Erbes*, 2015, Zürich: Edition Liberales Institut

Vaubel, Roland, the Role of Competition and in the Rise of Baroque and Renaissance Music, in: *Journal of Cultural Economics*, 2005, 29 (4), 277-97

Watson, Peter, *The German Genius. Europe's Third Renaissance, the Second Scientific Revolution and the Twentieth Century*, 2010, New York: Harper

Weede, Erich, Die Stellung Europas in der Welt, in: Pierre Bessard (Hrsg.), *Europa – Die Wiederentdeckung eines grossen Erbes*, 2015, Zürich: Edition Liberales Institut

Wohlgemuth, Michael, Liberale Perspektiven für die Europäische Union, in: Pierre Bessard (Hrsg.), *Europa – Die Wiederentdeckung eines großen Erbes*, 2015, Zürich: Edition Liberales Institut

Berkling, Kristof, Was uns die Geschichte der Mark Banco lehrt, 2013, http://www.misesde.org/?p=4014

Berschens, Ruth, Verschwendung von EU-Geldern, Finanzspritzen für Geisterhäfen, http://www.handelsblatt.com/politik/international/verschwendung-von-eu-geldern-finanzspritzen-fuergeisterhaefen/14589180.html

Bundesministerium der Finanzen, Der Finanzausgleich unter den Ländern für die Zeit vom 01.01.2015
–
31.12.2015, http://www.bundesfinanzministerium.de/Content/DE/Standardartikel/Themen/Oeffentliche_Finanzen/Fo Abrechnung-Laenderfinanzausgleich-2015.pdf?__blob=publicationFile&v=3

Durden, Tyler, Greenspan's Stunning Admission: »Gold Is Currency; No Fiat Currency, Including the Dollar, Can Match It«, http://www.zerohedge.com/news/2014-11-07/greenspans-stunning-admissiongold-currency-no-fiat-currency-including-dollar-can-ma

Eder, Florian, 4.365 EU-Beamte verdienen mehr als die Kanzlerin, https://www.welt.de/wirtschaft/article113330591/4365-EU-Beamte-verdienen-mehr-als-dieKanzlerin.html

Eder, Florian; Fründt, Steffen, Mit diesen Subventionen macht sich die EU lächerlich, https://www.welt.de/wirtschaft/article113327516/Mit-diesen-Subventionen-macht-sich-die-EUlaecherlich.html

Gammelin, Cerstin, Lobbyismus in Brüssel, Macht, Milliarden, Meinungsmacher, http://www.sueddeutsche.de/politik/lobbyismus-in-bruessel-macht-milliarden-meinungsmacher1.1957639

Gauck, Joachim im ARD-Interview »Bericht aus Berlin« mit Hassel, Tina, http://www.bundespraesident.de/SharedDocs/Reden/DE/Joachim-Gauck/Interviews/2016/160619Bericht-aus-Berlin-Interview.html

Gebel, Titus, Liechtenstein als Vorbild für Deutschland?, http://www.misesde.org/?p=14652

Groll, Tina, G20, Wirtschaftsmächte dringen auf strengere Steuerregeln für Konzerne, http://www.zeit.de/wirtschaft/2016-07/g20-finanzminister-steuerpolitik-finanztransaktionssteuer

Hayek, Friedrich August von, The Use of Knowledge in Society, https://fee.org/articles/the-use-ofknowledge-in-society/

Höltschi, René, Bilanz des EU-Südkorea-Abkommens, Eine Lanze für den Freihandel, http://www.nzz.ch/wirtschaft/wirtschaftspolitik/bilanz-des-eu-suedkorea-abkommens-eine-lanze-fuerden-freihandel-ld.103503

International Monetary Fund/Internationaler Währungsfonds, https://www.imf.org/external/

Losse, Bert, Inflation, Milliarden fürs Brot, http://www.wiwo.de/politik/konjunktur/inflationmilliarden-fuers-brot/7219052.html

Meyn, Charlotte Sophie, Kommt nach dem Brexit der Bayxit?, http://www.faz.net/aktuell/politik/brexit/kommt-nach-dem-brexit-der-bayxit-14337166.html

Pauker, Benjamin, Epiphanies from Nassim Nicholas Taleb, http://foreignpolicy.com/2012/10/08/epiphanies-from-nassim-nicholas-taleb/

Polleit, Thorsten, Fiskalpolitik: ›Keynesianer‹ versus ›Austrians‹, 2016, http://www.misesde.org/?p=12875

Rompuy, Herman Van; Barroso, José Manuel Durao, Vom Krieg zum Frieden – eine europäische Geschichte, Dankesrede zur Verleihung des Friedensnobelpreises® an die Europäische Union, https://europa.eu/european-union/sites/europaeu/files/docs/body/npp2013_de.pdf

SIPRI Milex data 1988–2015, https://www.sipri.org/sites/default/files/Milex-constant-USD.pdf

Statista – Das Statistik-Portal, https://de.statista.com/

# ABOUT THE AUTHORS

**Andreas Marquart** is a member of the board of the Ludwig-von-MisesInstitute in Germany. After graduating from high school, he completed a classic banking education. In 1998, after 15 years as a financial service banker, with a focus on asset investment, he became self-employed. He bases his life advice on the findings of the Austrian School of Economics. More about him can be found at: http://austrianconsult.de.

**Philipp Bagus** is Professor of Economics at the Universidad Rey Juan Carlos in Madrid. He has published articles in international journals such as the *Journal of Business Ethics, Independent Review* and *the American Journal of Economics and Sociology*. His work has been awarded the "O.P. Alford III Prize in Libertarian Scholarship," the "Sir John M. Templeton Fellowship," the "IREF Essay Prize" and the "Ron Paul Liberty in Media Award." He was also a recipient of the "Ludwig Erhard Award for Economy Journalism in 2016". His book *The Tragedy of the Euro* (FinanzBuch Publishing) was translated into 13 languages. With David Howden, he also published the book *Deep Freeze: Iceland's Economic Collapse*.

www.ingramcontent.com/pod-product-compliance
Lightning Source LLC
Chambersburg PA
CBHW020321290526
45785CB00007B/2872